100 I
Asked Questions
on the
ISO 9000:2000
Series

Also available from ASQ Quality Press:

The ASQ ISO 9000 Handbook
Charles A. Cianfrani, Joseph J. Tsiakals, and John E. (Jack) West

ISO 9001:2000 Explained, Second Edition
Joseph J. Tsiakals, Charles A. Cianfrani, and John E. (Jack) West

Quality Audits for ISO 9001:2000: Making Compliance Value-Added
Timothy O'Hanlon

ISO 9000:2000 Quick Reference
Jeanne Ketola and Kathy Roberts

ISO Lesson Guide 2000: Pocket Guide to Q9001:2000, Second Edition
Dennis Arter and J. P. Russell

ANSI/ISO/ASQ Q9000:2000 Series Quality Standards

ISO 9000:2000 for Small and Medium Businesses
Herb Monnich

The ISO 9001:2000 Auditor's Companion
Kent A. Keeney

The Practical Guide to People-Friendly Documentation
Adrienne Escoe

ISO 9001:2000 Revision Highlights: A Comparative Guide
Klaus Graebig

To request a complimentary catalog of ASQ Quality Press publications, call 800-248-1946, or visit our Web site at http://qualitypress.asq.org .

100 Frequently Asked Questions on the ISO 9000:2000 Series

Louise Bergenhenegouwen,
Annemarie de Jong,
and Henk J. de Vries

ASQ Quality Press
Milwaukee, Wisconsin

100 Frequently Asked Questions on the ISO 9000:2000 Series
Louise Bergenhenegouwen, Annemarie de Jong, and Henk J. de Vries

Library of Congress Cataloging-in-Publication Data

Bergenhenegouwen, Louise, 1972–
  100 frequently asked questions on the ISO 9000:2000 series / Louise
Bergenhenegouwen, Annemarie de Jong, and Henk J. de Vries.
    p. cm.
  ISBN 0-87389-541-X
  1. Quality control. 2. Total quality management. 3. Quality
control—Standards. I. Title: One hundred frequently asked questions on
the ISO 9000:2000 series. II. Jong, Annmarie de, 1953– III. Vries, Henk
J. de. IV. Title.

  TS156 .B4657 2002
  658.5'62—dc21   2002000402

ISBN 0-87389-541-X

Acquisitions Editor: Annemieke Koudstaal
Production Editor: Craig S. Powell
Production Administrator: Gretchen Trautman
Special Marketing Representative: Denise M. Cawley

ASQ Mission: The American Society for Quality advances individual,
organizational, and community excellence worldwide through learning, quality
improvement, and knowledge exchange.

Attention Bookstores, Wholesalers, Schools, and Corporations: ASQ Quality
Press books, videotapes, audiotapes, and software are available at quantity
discounts with bulk purchases for business, educational, or instructional use.
For information, please contact ASQ Quality Press at 800-248-1946, or write to
ASQ Quality Press, P.O. Box 3005, Milwaukee, WI 53201-3005.

To place orders or to request a free copy of the ASQ Quality Press Publications
Catalog, including ASQ membership information, call 800-248-1946. Visit our
Web site at www.asq.org or http://qualitypress.asq.org .

Printed in the United States of America

 Printed on acid-free paper

American Society for Quality
ASQ

Quality Press
600 N. Plankinton Avenue
Milwaukee, Wisconsin 53203
Call toll free 800-248-1946
Fax 414-272-1734
www.asq.org
http://qualitypress.asq.org
http://standardsgroup.asq.org
E-mail: authors@asq.org

This publication is a translation of the original Dutch publication *De 100 meest gestelde vragen over de nieuwe ISO 9000-serie.*

Nederlands Normalisatie-instituut
Postbus 5059
2600 GB Delft
Telephone +31 (0) 15 269 03 90
Fax +31 (0) 15 269 0190
Internet: http://www.nen.nl

For further information:
Netherlands Standardization Institute
NEN Consulting Services Management Systems
Telephone +31 (0) 15 269 02 89
Fax +31 (0) 15 269 02 07
e-mail: expertpunt@nen.nl

Note: As used in this document, the term "ISO 9000:2000" and all derivatives refer to the ANSI/ISO/ASQ Q9000-2000 series of documents. All quotations come from the American National Standard adoptions of these International Standards.

Table of Contents

Preface

The ISO 9000 series of 1994 has been revised and replaced by the ISO 9000:2000 series, published on December 15, 2000. The new series includes ISO 9000:2000, ISO 9001:2000, and ISO 9004:2000. The revision of the quality management systems standards raises questions in the minds of many users. Questions such as: What are the most important changes in the ISO 9000 series? What are the consequences for my quality management system? How much time remains to adapt the quality management system? From what date is it possible to obtain certification according to the new standard?

The answers to these and many other questions can be found in this publication. This guide is written for quality managers in organizations but can also be used by consultants, auditors, and teachers. You are given answers to questions about the content of the new ISO 9000 series and to questions about related matters such as certification and the transition period. This guide makes the transition to the new ISO 9000 standards much easier.

Most of the questions in this guide have been received by NEN Consulting Services Management Systems (Expertpunt Managementsystemen) at the Netherlands Standardization Institute. The experts at NEN Consulting Services Management

Systems are closely involved in the development of standards in the field of management systems. They provide support to the standardization committees for quality, occupational health and safety, and environmental management. Thanks to participation in this network they are fully aware of the standards.

We would like to thank a few people explicitly. In compiling this guide we have received many valuable suggestions from:

- Ir. B. Alisic, senior manager KPMG Management Consulting N.V., expert in the ISO working group for ISO 9001 and 9004

- Ing. W. J. Bosman, management consultant KIWA N.V., member of the Dutch translation task group

- Ing. B. Kornelisse, consultancy director Bureau Veritas, expert in the ISO working group for ISO 19011 on auditing

- Prof.ir. N. van Omme, former lecturer in quality management at the University of Groningen

Mr. F. G. A. J. M. Geertsen, expert in the international (ISO) working group for quality management principles, also deserves our sincere thanks. All are members of the Dutch standardization committee on quality management.

We are also grateful to have been able to make use of the knowledge, experience, and input of our closest colleagues in NEN Consulting Services Management Systems, Dick Hortensius and Eva Kosto.

We anticipate that the ISO 9000:2000 series, in combination with the explanations in this publication, will help you with the structured improvement of your business management. We wish you every success in adapting your quality management system to the new requirements of ISO 9001:2000.

Louise Bergenhenegouwen
Annemarie de Jong
Henk J. de Vries

Introduction

The ISO 9000:2000 series replaces the ISO 9000 series of 1994. The revision of these quality management systems standards has consequences for many organizations. Hundreds of thousands of organizations worldwide are working with ISO 9000 standards. At the end of 1999, the number of ISO 9000 certificates issued worldwide totaled 343,643, according to the ISO survey.

The revision of the ISO 9000 series has raised many questions. In this publication you can find specific questions about the new ISO 9000 series and their corresponding answers. But even if you do not have any specific questions, by reading this publication you will gain clear information on the ISO 9000:2000 series.

How to Read This Book

Chapter 1 discusses the structural changes of the ISO 9000 series. Chapter 2 discusses the changes in content. Chapter 3 addresses the basic principles of quality management. These eight quality management principles form the basis for the new ISO 9000 series. The titles and numbering of chapters 4 through 8 run parallel with the titles and numbering of clauses 4 through 8 of ISO 9001:2000, which makes it easier to find questions and answers regarding requirements in the standard. The subjects in clauses 4 through 8 come from the following model of a process-based quality management system that serves as a basis for ISO 9001:2000 and ISO 9004:2000:

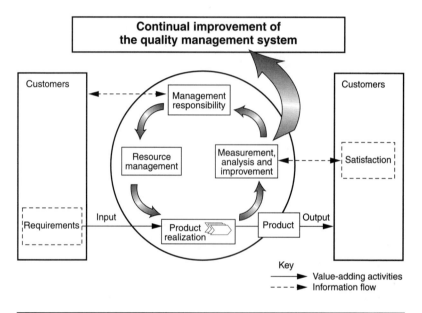

Model of a process-based quality management system.
Source: ANSI/ISO/ASQ Q9001-2000

On the left side you see the customer requirements—input for the organization—and on the right side—as an output—the products for which the customer (hopefully) shows their satisfaction. In between you see the organization continuously improving customer satisfaction. In the model of a process-based quality management system, four groups of processes are identified that together form a quality management system.

These four groups are, respectively:

- Management responsibility

- Resource management

- Product realization

- Measurement, analysis, and improvement

The four processes in this model form the key clauses—5, 6, 7, and 8—of both ISO 9001:2000 and ISO 9004:2000. You will find them as chapters 5, 6, 7, and 8 in this publication as well:

- Management responsibility (chapter 5)

- Resource management (chapter 6)

- Product realization (chapter 7)

- Measurement, analysis, and improvement (chapter 8)

The requirements of the quality management system itself are mentioned in clause 4 of ISO 9001:2000. The questions about this subject are answered in chapter 4 of this guide. Questions on certification and the transition period are covered in chapter 9. Finally, chapter 10 deals with a few other frequently asked questions covering a wide range of topics. Using the index you can easily find questions and their corresponding answers. In Appendix 1 you will find a list of the abbreviations used in this publication. Appendix 2 lists all the standards and guidelines in the ISO 9000 family. Appendices 3, 4, 5, and 6 contain cross-reference tables from the 1994 version to the 2000 version, and vice versa. These appendices also include cross-reference tables from the new ISO 9001 to ISO 14001:1996 for environmental management, and vice versa.

The Most Important Changes in the Structure and Coherence of the ISO 9000 Series

1. **What will be the structure of the new ISO 9000 series and what is its relationship to the other standards and guidelines in the ISO 9000 family?**

The ISO 9000 series is often confused with the ISO 9000 family. The ISO 9000 series forms the core of the ISO 9000 family and is comprised of:

- ISO 9000 *Quality management systems—Fundamentals and vocabulary*

- ISO 9001 *Quality management systems—Requirements*

- ISO 9004 *Quality management systems—Guidelines for performance improvements*

- ISO 19011 *Guidelines on quality and/or environmental management system auditing* (until its publication in 2002, guidelines on quality management system auditing can be found in ISO 10011 *Guidelines for auditing quality systems;* see also question 72)

The ISO 9000:2000 series replaces the following standards and guidelines:

- ISO 9000:2000 replaces:

  - ISO 9000-1 *Guidelines for selection and use*

  - ISO 8402 *Vocabulary*

- ISO 9001:2000 replaces:

  - ISO 9001 *Model for quality assurance in design, development, production, installation and servicing*

  - ISO 9002 *Model for quality assurance in production, installation and servicing*

  - ISO 9003 *Model for quality assurance in final inspection and test*

- ISO 9004:2000 replaces:

  - ISO 9004-1 *Quality management and quality system elements—Part 1: Guidelines*

As of December 15, 2000, the ISO 9000 group of standards still consisted of 20 standards and guidelines. In addition to those mentioned above, there are ISO 9000 standards that help interpret (ISO 9000-2 *Generic guidelines for the application of ISO 9001, ISO 9002 and ISO 9003)* and give guidance in applying the ISO 9000 series in different product categories:

- ISO 9000-3 for software

- ISO 9004-2 for services

- ISO 9004-3 for processed materials

In the ISO 9000 family you will also find guidelines for:

- Quality improvement (ISO 9004-4)

- Developing quality plans (ISO 10005)

- Project management (ISO 10006)

- Configuration management (ISO 10007)

- Control of measuring equipment (ISO 10012)

- Developing quality manuals (ISO 10013)

- Managing the economics of quality (ISO/TR 10014)

- Training (ISO 10015)

- Statistical techniques (ISO/TR 10017)

See Appendix 2 for a full list.

After the revision of the ISO 9000 series, many of these guidelines will be withdrawn as they are incorporated into the new ISO 9000:2000 series. Other guidelines are being incorporated in the long term, for example those in "Technical Reports" (TR) or brochures, so no valuable knowledge and information is being lost.

2. Why was the ISO 9000 series revised?

The main reason for the revision of the ISO 9000 series was the observed need for:

- Improved user-friendliness

- More attention to the process approach

- More attention to continual improvement

- More attention to resource management, including human resources

- Improved integration of quality management systems with other management systems, for example ISO 14001

- A better relationship between requirements for quality assurance (ISO 9001) and guidelines for improving performance (ISO 9004)

- The possibility for self-assessment for overall performance improvement

- Better application of general quality management principles in organizations

Extensive research has been carried out worldwide to investigate the needs of the users of quality management system standards and to list their experiences with these standards. The revision has been based on experience with the 1987 and 1994 standards. New points of view regarding management systems have also been taken into account.

3. Was there something wrong with the 1994 version of the ISO 9000 series?

The standards and guidelines from the ISO 9000 series have proven their value worldwide. Hundreds of thousands of enterprises use them. Almost 350,000 organizations worldwide are certified on the basis of ISO 9001, ISO 9002, or ISO 9003.

There has also been criticism. The most frequently heard criticism is that the application of standards leads to unnecessary bureaucracy. It cannot be denied that this happens in practice. The question is whether that is because of the standards themselves or the way in which they are applied. The following points of criticism are, in any case, justified:

- The structure of ISO 9001, with 20 paragraphs, does not focus enough on how processes are managed in organizations

- For organizations that do not make tangible products, such as service-providing organizations, the current standards are difficult to interpret. Think, for example, of an advertising bureau. How must subclause 4.11 "Control of inspection, measuring and test equipment" be interpreted? Does this involve control of the secretary's scales for weighing letters?

4. What happened to ISO 9002 and 9003?

As of December 15, 2000, distinctions between ISO 9001, ISO 9002, and ISO 9003 have disappeared. The 1994 standards ISO 9002 and ISO 9003 have been withdrawn, which means that organizations with a quality management system based on ISO 9002 or ISO 9003 have to use ISO 9001:2000. They must then indicate in the quality manual and on any certificate what the scope of the quality management system is. They may, for example, indicate in the scope that there are no design and development activities present, therefore they are not part of the quality management system. The new standard states that when any requirement cannot be applied due to the nature of an organization and its product, that requirement can be considered for exclusion. If you think that a requirement is not applicable, you must, if your organization wants to receive a certificate, provide sound arguments for this to the certification body (see also question 73).

5. What requirements of ISO 9000:2000 can I exclude?

Any requirement that cannot be applied due to the nature of an organization and its product can be considered for exclusion.

Exclusion may not affect the organization's ability, or responsibility, to provide products that fulfill customer and applicable regulatory requirements. Exclusions are limited to the requirements within clause 7, *Product realization,* of ISO 9001:2000. In view of the relatively large number of ISO 9002:1994 certificates at present, it is anticipated that mainly requirements for design and development activities will be excluded (see also questions 73–75).

6. When was the new ISO 9000 series published?

Publication of the new ISO 9000 series was on December 15, 2000. This is the date that the transition period started (see also questions 78–80). Since then, many translations in national languages have been published. ISO 19011 is scheduled for publication in 2002.

7. Why are translations of the ISO 9000 series released later than the internationally published series?

Translating is difficult. English terms like *management* or *monitoring* can be translated in many ways. The final national editions can only be prepared when the final English texts are available. The translation has to be approved by the national quality management standardization committee of each particular country. In addition, agreement may be necessary with same-language-speaking countries so that there is only one authorized translation for one language-speaking region.

8. Why do ISO standards have different designations in different countries?

The status of approval is indicated by various designations. "ISO" is the designation for standards developed by ISO (International Organization for Standardization—see question 95). The letters "EN" (European standard) indicate that the standard has also been adopted at the European level, namely by the European Standardization Institute CEN (Comité Européen de Normalisation).

The standardization bodies in the countries of the European Union, Iceland, Norway, the Czech Republic, and Switzerland have agreed that they will adopt European standards unchanged into their national standards system. Countries in the European Union have their own national designation when the standard is published (and possibly also translated) on a national level. For example in the Netherlands this is indicated by adding the letters "NEN."

9. Why has the ISO 9000 series also become an American National Standard?

International standards are adopted as American National Standards if they are considered to be sufficiently important for the American market. Commercial transactions must not be hindered by differences in national standards. Should there be national standards that differ from the international standard, these must be withdrawn. Most standards from the ISO 9000 family are important in commercial transactions and are therefore adopted as American National Standards.

Major Changes to the Content of the ISO 9000 Series

10. **How does the basis of the 1994 ISO 9000 series differ in content from that of 2000?**

The ISO 9000:2000 series has *improving customer satisfaction* as a new measurement of performance of the quality management system. The 1994 version was also aimed at satisfying the customer, but less explicitly: via meeting product requirements. The new ISO 9000 series adds the element *enhancing customer satisfaction.* A mechanism has also been built in requiring continual improvement of the effectiveness of the quality management system.

Another important difference between the 1994 version and the 2000 version is that the new ISO 9000 series is based on a process approach. The new version more strongly recommends a process approach to quality management systems.

Finally, the ISO 9000:2000 series considers eight quality management principles as a basic philosophy (see chapter 3). These principles are, in part, identifiable in ISO 9001:2000, but more so in ISO 9004:2000.

11. How does ISO 9001:2000 differ from ISO 9001:1994?

The main differences between ISO 9001:2000 and ISO 9001:1994 are:

- Enhancing customer satisfaction is seen as a measurement of performance of the quality management system

- A process approach to quality management systems is important

- The responsibility of top management has become more important, certainly with respect to enhancing customer satisfaction

- Attention to resources (both human and non-human factors)

- Emphasis on continual improvement of the effectiveness of the quality management system

12. How does ISO 9004:2000 differ from ISO 9004:1994?

ISO 9004-1:1994 was supplemented by:

- ISO 9004-2:1991 for services

- ISO 9004-3:1993 for processed materials

- ISO 9004-4:1993 for quality improvement

ISO 9004:2000 replaces ISO 9004-1. For the time being, ISO 9004-2, ISO 9004-3, and ISO 9004-4 are maintained.

ISO 9000-3 for the application of ISO 9001:1994 to software is *not* being replaced, but remains in existence. The new ISO 9004:2000 applies to all organizations, irrespective of the type of product that they supply. *Products* also include services (see question 19). Just like the standards of 1994, ISO 9004:2000 offers guidelines for quality management systems. These new guidelines, however, go further. Important innovations are:

- ISO 9004:2000 is aimed at enhancing satisfaction of all interested parties (customers and other interested parties, such as shareholders, employees, and so on)

- ISO 9004:2000 is aimed at continual improvement of the organization's overall performance, effectiveness, and efficiency measured through the satisfaction of customers and other interested parties

- The guidelines of ISO 9004:2000 now link up perfectly with the firm requirements in ISO 9001:2000

- ISO 9004:2000 now has a more logical structure, similar to that of ISO 9001:2000

- ISO 9004:2000 reflects the latest internationally recognized points of view on quality management systems and can form a bridge between ISO 9001 and quality award models

- Organizations can use ISO 9004:2000 for self-assessment (Annex A in ISO 9004:2000 is a practical aid for this)

- The ISO 9004:2000 guidelines are now based on eight quality management principles (see chapter 3)

13. What is the relationship between ISO 9001:2000 and ISO 9004:2000?

ISO 9001:2000 and ISO 9004:2000 are intended to be used in combination, but you can also apply them independently of each other. They have similar structures in order to assist their application as a consistent pair.

ISO 9001:2000 specifies requirements for a quality management system that can be used for internal application, for contractual use, or for certification. It focuses on the effectiveness of the quality management system in meeting customer requirements in order to enhance customer satisfaction. When measures to comply with ISO 9001:2000 are introduced in your organization, you can go a step beyond by applying the guidelines of ISO 9004:2000 as well. ISO 9004:2000 contains guidelines for a quality management system that has the aim of improving the overall performance and capabilities of an organization. ISO 9004:2000 contains guidelines for improving processes that are not mission-critical yet enhance customer satisfaction. Hence, ISO 9004:2000 provides a wider range of objectives for a quality management system than ISO 9001 has for the performance of the quality management system, namely, in addition to the customer, other interested parties (such as shareholders, employees, and so on) are addressed. ISO 9004:2000 is not intended for certification or contractual purposes. By first meeting the requirements of ISO 9001:2000 and then paying attention to less critical processes (less critical in relation to customer satisfaction) and to all interested parties (not only the customer), you work increasingly in accordance with principles of business excellence or total quality management (see Figure 2.1).

The following is an example to clarify the relationship between ISO 9001, ISO 9004, and business excellence.

Imagine you are a hairdresser and you work in accordance with the requirements of the new ISO 9001. Your customers can assume from this that their hair will be cut and styled in such a way that they will go home satisfied with their new hairdo. After all, you meet the requirements of the new ISO 9001, so you try to enhance customer satisfaction by meeting their requirements.

However, when you go a step beyond by taking into account interested parties other than just customers and by improving processes that are less critical for the quality of the product, you are involved in quality management as intended in the new ISO 9004. If, for example, your employees get skin irritation from certain shampoos, you can replace these with shampoos that do not cause irritation and are also environmentally friendly. Assuming that the change to different shampoos does not affect the quality of the hairdo, you are improving a process that is not critical for enhancing customer satisfaction, but that does contribute to improving the overall performance of your hairdresser's shop.

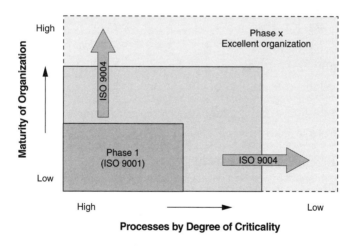

Figure 2.1 Using ISO 9001 and ISO 9004 to achieve business excellence.

PROCESS APPROACH

14. How is the process approach integrated into ISO 9001:2000 and ISO 9004:2000?

Both ISO 9001:2000 and ISO 9004:2000 are, in order to guarantee a process approach, based on a specially developed model. This model of a process-based quality management system represents the philosophy behind the standards. The model is based on customer requirements as input. These requirements are transformed into a product (output) that, hopefully, enhances customer satisfaction. This transformation involves the integration of four processes:

- Management, for which top management is responsible

- Resource management

- Product realization

- Measurement, analysis, and improvement

These four processes in the model form the four key clauses. The model shown in Figure 2.2 covers all the requirements of the International Standard (IS), but does not show processes at the detailed level of both ISO 9001:2000 and ISO 9004:2000. You will find them as chapters 5, 6, 7, and 8 in this publication:

- Management responsibility (chapter 5)

- Resource management (chapter 6)

- Product realization (chapter 7)

- Measurement, analysis, and improvement (chapter 8)

The requirements for the quality management system itself are mentioned in clause 4 of ISO 9001:2000. The questions on this subject are answered in chapter 4 of this guide.

Note that the models in ISO 9001:2000 and ISO 9004:2000 differ slightly: ISO 9004:2000 focuses on the satisfaction of "interested parties" instead of the satisfaction of "customers."

15. What does the model of a process-based quality management system look like?

The model of ISO 9001:2000 appears as follows:

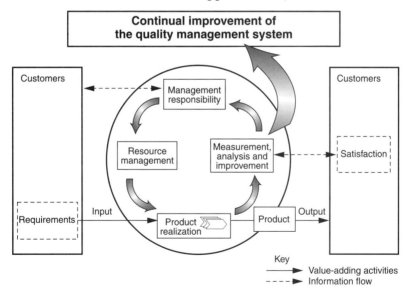

Figure 2.2 Model of a process-based quality management system.
Source: ANSI/ISO/ASQ Q9001-2000

The customer requirements are the inputs for product realization. The output of this (the product) is supplied to the customer and must enhance customer satisfaction by meeting customer requirements. Customer satisfaction results from the customer's perception as to whether the organization has met his or her requirements. To make this possible, product realization is controlled. Top management, by managing resources, must ensure that the organization is able to realize products that meet customer requirements. (The reverse is also true: the organization must only take on commitments if it knows that it can meet the requirements).

The quality of the processes, the product, and customer satisfaction must be measured and then analyzed. If there are differences between results achieved and results desired, corrective action must be taken. (Preventive action must eliminate causes of possible nonconformities, to prevent failure of the organization). Monitoring of customer satisfaction requires the evaluation of information relating to customer perception as to whether the organization has met customer requirements. The difference between desired and achieved performance forms the basis for continual improvement of the effectiveness of the quality management system. Hence, the matching of the organization with the requirements of the customer can be better carried out in the future. Top management is responsible for the development and implementation of the quality management system and for the continual improvement of its effectiveness.

16. Why has the title of ISO 9001:2000 been revised?

The new version of ISO 9001 has a revised title in which the term *quality assurance,* from the 1994 version, no longer appears. The reason for this is that the quality management system requirements specified in the new version of ISO 9001 address both quality assurance of product and customer satisfaction (ANSI/ISO/ASQ Q9001-2000, Foreword). In the run-up to the revision process the distinction between *quality assurance* (ISO 9001) and *quality management* (ISO 9004) was still used. This caused a lot of discussion and confusion, however, about the distinction between these two terms. A very common misconception was that quality assurance stood alongside quality management as something different.

In ISO 9000:2000, *quality assurance* is defined as a part of quality management, focused on providing confidence that quality requirements will be fulfilled. The other parts of quality management are: quality planning, quality control, and quality improvement. ISO 9001 contains requirements for all these matters. Other fundamentally important changes relate to the terms *quality, supplier,* and *product.* Questions 17, 18, and 19 explain these terms.

17. What is the meaning of the term *quality* in ISO 9000:2000?

In ISO 9000:2000, the meaning of the term *quality* is the "degree to which a set of inherent characteristics fulfills requirements" (ANSI/ISO/ASQ Q9000-2000, para. 3.1.1). The term *quality* can be used with adjectives such as poor, good, or excellent. *Inherent,* as opposed to *assigned,* means existing in something, especially as a permanent characteristic. *Requirements* are needs or expectations of customers and other interested parties, whether stated, generally implied, or obligatory. In ISO 9000:2000, the term *quality,* just like other important terms, is explained with a concept diagram. Concept diagrams show relations between terms in a graphic way. The term *quality* is shown in a concept diagram (Figure 2.3).

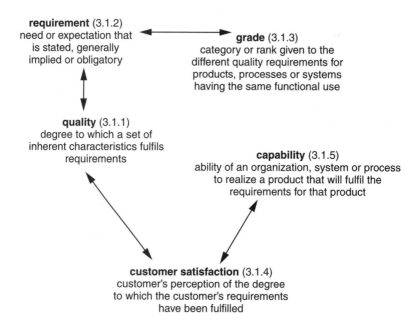

requirement (3.1.2)
need or expectation that
is stated, generally
implied or obligatory

grade (3.1.3)
category or rank given to the
different quality requirements for
products, processes or systems
having the same functional use

quality (3.1.1)
degree to which a set of
inherent characteristics fulfils
requirements

capability (3.1.5)
ability of an organization, system or process
to realize a product that will fulfil the
requirements for that product

customer satisfaction (3.1.4)
customer's perception of the degree
to which the customer's requirements
have been fulfilled

Figure 2.3   Concepts relating to quality.
Source: ANSI/ISO/ASQ Q9000-2000, Annex A, Figure A.4

18. How does the term *supplier* change?

The term *supplier* has changed in ISO 9000:2000. In the 1994 version of the standards your own organization is called *supplier.* You supply to a *customer* and buy from a *subcontractor:*

subcontractor → supplier → customer (1994 version)

In the new standards, your own organization (the unit to which the International Standard applies) is called *organization,* you supply to a *customer,* and buy from a *supplier:*

supplier → organization → customer (2000 version)

19. What does the term *product* mean in ISO 9000:2000?

The term *product* in ISO 9000:2000 means the result of a process. Products can also mean services. Where the standard talks about *product,* it covers four product categories or combinations thereof (ANSI/ISO/ASQ Q9000-2000, para. 3.4.2). The following example of an automobile shows the difference between the four product categories:

Product Category	Example: Automobile
Hardware	Tires, motor components
Processed materials	Fuel, cooling liquid
Software	Driver's manual, engine control software
Services	Operating explanations given by the salesman

Whether combined products are designated as hardware, processed materials, software, or services depends on the dominant element. Automobiles are hardware, transport is service—although vehicles (hardware) are used for this.

20. What are the quality management system principles on which the new ISO 9000 series is based?

In the case of quality management in accordance with the ISO 9000 series, the following eight principles are involved:

- Customer-focused organization

- Leadership

- Involvement of people

- Process approach

- System approach to management
- Continual improvement
- Factual approach to decision making
- Mutually beneficial supplier relationships

See also chapter 3 of this book.

Quality Management Principles

21. What is a quality management principle?

A quality management principle is a universal and fundamental rule or belief for leading and operating an organization, aimed at helping users achieve organizational success. Systematic application of all eight principles provides *total quality.* The quality management principles form the basic philosophy behind the new ISO 9000 standards. Some of the principles can be found in ISO 9001:2000; all the principles are used in ISO 9004:2000.

22. Why have the quality management principles been established?

The quality management principles have been established to help organizations with quality management systems form a basis for performance improvement and organizational excellence. Organizations that fully apply these principles go beyond the *minimum level* of ISO 9001:2000 (which of course is already higher than that of ISO 9001:1994). Because the quality management principles form the basis of ISO 9004:2000, this guideline has a wider range of objectives than ISO 9004:1994 (see question 12). The principles reflect the joint knowledge and experience of leading experts from 46 countries. They are considered valuable and can be applied in many cultures (the worldwide applicability and recognition naturally also apply for ISO 9001:2000 and the other ISO 9000 standards and guidelines).

23. What does principle 1, *customer-focused organization*, mean?

Organizations depend on their customers and therefore should understand current and future customer needs, should meet customer requirements, and strive to exceed customer expectations (ANSI/ISO/ASQ Q9004-2000, para. 4.3).

This can be done by:

- Researching the multitude of needs and expectations of the different types of customers regarding the specific activities of the organization

- Linking objectives of the organization with these needs and expectations

- Ensuring that these needs and expectations are known and understood throughout the organization

- Measuring customer satisfaction and acting on the results

- Systematically managing customer relationships

- Finding a well-balanced approach between customers and other interested parties

ANSI/ISO/ASQ Q9001-2000 (para. 5.2) states that top management shall ensure that customer requirements are determined and are met with the aim of enhancing customer satisfaction.

The following example illustrates the principle of customer focus. A nursing home has a system in which the residents receive a standard portion of sandwiches in their room each day. Being aware of the principle of customer focus leads one to ask the question, "If I lived here, would I like it if other people decided how many sandwiches I should have, and what kind?" Applying the principle of customer focus resulted in a built-in shop with a coffee corner, a restaurant facility in the dining room, hexagonal tables, and serving lessons for the personnel. Consequence: more social contact between the residents and a considerable improvement in the atmosphere.

This example shows that you not only have to do what the client explicitly asks for, you must take active steps to put yourself in the customer's position to find out what their explicit and implicit wishes and needs are. These wishes and needs not only relate to the product itself, but also, for example, to the delivery, price, and service relating to the product (see also questions 32, 33, and 41–44).

LEADERSHIP

24. What does principle 2, *leadership*, mean?

Leaders establish unity of purpose and direction of the organization. They should create and maintain the internal environment in which people can become fully involved in achieving the organization's objectives.

This may be done by, among other things:

- Considering the needs of all interested parties including customers, owners, employees, suppliers, local communities, and society in general

- Establishing a clear vision of the organization's future

- Setting challenging goals and targets

- Creating and sustaining shared values, fairness, and ethical role models at all levels of the organization

- Establishing trust and eliminating fear

- Providing people with the required resources, training, and freedom to act with responsibility and accountability

- Inspiring and encouraging people to contribute to the proper functioning of the organization, and then recognizing these contributions

See also questions 41, 42, and 47.

25. Is there a particular management theory for principle 2 on leadership?

No, the committee that drafted the principles expressed no preference for a particular management theory. It is clear, however, that not all styles of leadership match with this principle equally well. Authoritarian leadership, for example, does not fit in with it because, generally speaking, it is not very stimulating for the employees. The reverse is also possible, as the following example illustrates:

A big printing company got a new director. He regularly visited the night shift unexpectedly. He brought them snacks and coffee. They ate together and talked about the work. The people very much welcomed these unexpected visits: the director was interested in their work. The director got good ideas for improvements from the night shift. Their productivity increased by some 35% after a couple of months.

This example shows how essential good leadership can be in achieving effective and efficient management.

26. What does principle 3, *involvement of people*, mean?

People at all levels are the essence of an organization and their full involvement enables their abilities to be used for the organization's benefit. Applying the principle of *involvement of people* typically leads to people who:

- Understand the importance of their contribution and role in the organization

- Identify constraints to their performance

- Accept ownership and responsibility for solving problems

- Evaluate their own performance against personal goals and objectives

- Actively seek opportunities to enhance their competency, knowledge, and experience

- Freely share knowledge and experience

- Openly discuss problems and issues

If you choose to give more responsibility and authority to those who work in operating processes, you can translate the general objectives of your organization via department objectives and individual objectives. If necessary, you can link compensation to the achievement of individual objectives. The example in question 25 shows how involvement of employees can be obtained and what involvement can provide. See also question 54.

27. What does principle 4, *process approach*, mean?

A desired result is achieved more efficiently when activities and related resources are managed as a process.

Any activity using resources and managed in order to enable the transformation of inputs into outputs can be considered as a process. Oftentimes, the output from one process directly forms the input to the next process. The application of a system of processes within an organization, together with the identification and interactions of these processes, and their management, can be referred to as the *process approach* (ANSI/ISO/ASQ Q9001-2000, para. 0.2). The process approach means the following, among other things:

- Using structured methods to define the activities necessary to obtain the desired result

- Establishing clear responsibility and accountability for managing key activities (by appointing a [sub-]process owner)

- Identifying the various inputs and outputs for each activity, indicating what requirements these must meet, and assessing whether they meet these requirements

- Identifying interfaces and interactions between the different activities

- Focusing on the factors, such as resources, methods, and materials needed to be able to carry out and improve the activities

- Evaluating possible risks in processes, and the consequences and impacts on customers, suppliers, and other interested parties

An advantage of the process approach is the ongoing control that it provides over the linkage between the individual processes within the system, as well as over their combination and interaction.

See also question 15.

SYSTEM APPROACH TO MANAGEMENT

28. What does principle 5, *system approach to management,* mean?

Identifying, understanding, and managing interrelated processes as a system contributes to the organization's effectiveness and efficiency in achieving its objectives.

The so-called *system approach to management* may, among other things, include the following measures:

- Structuring and implementing a system to achieve the organization's objectives in the most effective and efficient way

- Understanding the interdependencies among the processes of the system

- Providing a better understanding of the roles and responsibilities necessary for achieving common objectives, thereby reducing cross-functional barriers

- Understanding organizational capabilities and establishing resource constraints prior to action

- Targeting and defining how specific activities within a system should operate

- Continually improving the system based on measurements and analysis of the results

29. What does principle 6, *continual improvement,* mean?

Continual improvement of the organization's overall performance should be a permanent objective of the organization.

Application of the principle of continual improvement means, among other things:

- Employing a consistent organizationwide approach to continual improvement

- Training employees in the use of methods and tools for continual improvement

- Making continual improvement of products, processes, and systems an objective for everyone in the organization

- Establishing goals to guide, and measures to track, continual improvements

- Recognizing and acknowledging improvements

See also question 66.

FACTUAL APPROACH TO DECISION MAKING

30. What does principle 7, *factual approach to decision making,* mean?

Effective decisions are based on the analysis of data and information. Application of this principle means, among other things, that you ensure the generation of data and information that are sufficiently accurate and reliable, and are accessible to those who have to use them. This principle also means that decisions and actions are based on factual analyses balanced with experience and intuition.

31. What does principle 8, *mutually beneficial supplier relationships,* mean?

An organization and its suppliers are interdependent. A mutually beneficial relationship enhances the ability of both to create value.

MUTUALLY BENEFICIAL SUPPLIER
RELATIONSHIPS

Mutually beneficial supplier relationships may, for example, arise from:

- Carefully identifying and selecting key suppliers
- Developing relationships with suppliers that balance short-term gains with long-term considerations
- Pooling of expertise and resources with key partners
- Clear and open communications
- Sharing information and future plans
- Establishing joint development and improvement activities
- Inspiring, encouraging, and recognizing improvements and achievements

Good cooperation can result in lower costs and other benefits for both parties. Once one of the parties has the feeling that the other is exploiting him or "bleeding him dry," the partnership is already undermined and there is no mutually beneficial relationship.

32. What is the relationship between the quality management principles and ISO 9001:2000?

The application of quality management principles may contribute to continual improvement of the quality management system and, hence, to improving the overall performance of the organization. You can apply the quality management principles in various ways. How depends on the nature of your organization and the specific circumstances you have to deal with. If you want to implement these principles in your organization, you can introduce a quality management system that is based on these principles. The standards and guidelines from the ISO 9000 series, in particular ISO 9004:2000, will help you. Those parts of the principles that are most important to your customers can be found in ISO 9001. If your quality management system complies with ISO 9001:2000, your organization is able to manage elementary customer-focused processes so that customer satisfaction can be enhanced systematically.

33. Can I comply with ISO 9001:2000 without adhering to quality management principles?

ISO 9001 does not require that you use the principles for quality management. The principles, however, have formed a basis for the requirements of ISO 9001, even though all eight are not expressed to the same extent in this standard. This is particularly true for the principles of customer focus, process approach, and system approach to management. It is easier to work in accordance with the requirements and philosophy of ISO 9001 if you are familiar with the principles and understand what they would mean in your own organization.

Quality Management System

34. Should I base my quality management system on the model of a process-based system?

Although ISO 9001:2000 is structured according to the model of a process-based quality management system, it does not necessarily imply that you need to design your quality management system according to this model. The model is described in the standard's introduction. The real requirements start in ISO 9001:2000, clause 4. The general requirements oblige you to:

- Identify processes

- Determine their sequence and interaction

- Determine the criteria and methods for their effective operation and control

- Ensure the availability of resources and information necessary to support the operation and monitoring of these processes

- Monitor, measure, and analyze these processes

- Implement actions necessary to achieve planned results and continual improvement of these processes

- Manage these processes in accordance with the requirements of ISO 9001:2000

Source: ANSI/ISO/ASQ Q9001-2000, para. 4.1.

35. Is outsourcing of quality-related processes allowed?

Yes, you can outsource a process that affects the conformity of a product to the requirements, but your organization shall ensure control over such processes. Your quality management system must identify how outsourced processes are controlled (ANSI/ISO/ASQ Q9001-2000, para. 4.1).

36. Is anything changing in the quality manual, procedures, instructions, or other documentation?

For some organizations nothing changes, for others quite a lot. If in your quality management system you have arranged the documentation in accordance with the structure of the paragraphs in ISO 9001:1994 (function-oriented quality management system), a lot has to change. The paragraph layout in ISO 9001:1994 has been turned completely upside down—the new standard has a more logical layout. Even more important is the fact that the new standard is based on a process approach (see the answer to question 15). Quite naturally, you structure your quality management system and the corresponding documentation on the basis of your business processes (process-based quality management system), not on the basis of the requirements in the standard. If you choose to have an alternative structure, however, you can always refer in your documentation to the relevant paragraphs of ISO 9001:2000. That will be useful for internal and/or external audits.

The requirements for document control have changed in ISO 9001:2000. The standard still indicates that in a number of cases you must establish documented procedures. In general, documented procedures that are necessary for effective implementation and control of quality management system processes are required. For some subjects, procedures are not required anymore (see question 38). In general, the new standard is less prescriptive than the 1994 version and allows an organization more flexibility in the way it chooses to document its quality management system. This enables each individual organization to develop the minimum amount of documentation needed in order to demonstrate the effective planning, operation, and control of its processes and the implementation and continual improvement of its quality management system. ISO 9001:2000 contains a new requirement about the quality manual. You must indicate in it the scope of the quality management system. If you exclude parts of the standard (see questions 5 and 73–75), you must provide details to the certification body or the customer of what has been excluded and why (ANSI/ISO/ASQ Q9001-2000, para. 4.2.2). Finally, there is the new requirement that you must describe the sequence and interaction between processes in the quality management system.

37. Can I operate using fewer procedures?

ISO 9001:2000 still explicitly requires that procedures are necessary for some activities. For other activities procedures are not explicitly required. In total, six documented procedures are mandatory in addition to other documents in the quality management system (see question 38). The central criterion is whether the procedures are necessary for managing processes that are critical for meeting customer requirements. In cases of stringent customer requirements, more procedures may be necessary than when the requirement level is lower. For complex or risky realization processes, more procedures are usually anticipated than in the case of simple and risk-avoiding processes. Another criterion for the necessity of documented procedures is the effective implementation and control of processes. This does not mean that in cases of critical situations documented procedures are always the right remedy. A lot can be accomplished by training personnel. In a surgical ward at a hospital, the processes are very critical, but documented procedures are not very practical. In practice, however, doctors and nurses do know precisely what they must do and follow the procedures in this way. Para. 4.2.1 of ANSI/ISO/ASQ Q9001-2000 also states that the extent of the documentation for the quality management system (hence also the required procedures) depends on:

- The size of the organization and type of activities

- The complexity of processes and their interactions

- The competence of personnel

By paying more explicit attention to processes, procedures will also focus more on the processes than on functional departments. This generally reduces the number of procedures required, as each department no longer has its own procedures. In short, the number of procedures differs for each organization, depending on:

- Size and type of the organization

- Risk of the processes

- Complexity of, and interactions between, the business processes

- Competence of personnel

- Level of customer requirements

- Degree to which the documentation of the quality management system is process-related

See also questions 36 and 38.

38. What documented procedures and documents are mandatory?

ISO 9001:2000 requires documented procedures for:

- Control of documents (ANSI/ISO/ASQ Q9001-2000, para. 4.2.3)

- Control of records (ANSI/ISO/ASQ Q9001-2000, para. 4.2.4)

- Internal audits (ANSI/ISO/ASQ Q9001-2000, para. 8.2.2)

- Control of nonconformity (ANSI/ISO/ASQ Q9001-2000, para. 8.3)

- Corrective action (ANSI/ISO/ASQ Q9001-2000, para. 8.5.2)

- Preventive action (ANSI/ISO/ASQ Q9001-2000, para. 8.5.3)

Where the standard specifically requires a documented procedure, the procedure has to be established, documented, implemented, and maintained. See also questions 36 and 37.

In order for an organization to demonstrate the effective implementation of its quality management system, it must develop more documents than just documented procedures.

The documents specifically mentioned in ANSI/ISO/ASQ
Q 9001-2000 are (para. 4.2.1):

- A quality policy

- Quality objectives

- A quality manual

- Documented procedures required by the
  International Standard

- Documents needed to ensure the effective planning,
  operation, and control of its processes

- Records required by the International Standard

39. How can I convert a function-based quality management system into a process-based quality management system?

For a process-based quality management system it is important
to use the *critical* operational company processes and the way
these processes are now controlled as a starting point. The following steps can be used:

Step 1:   *Get an understanding of the essence of
            ISO 9001:2000.* Look at the requirements of the
            new ISO 9001 in order to understand the essence
            of these requirements, but do not go into the details.

Step 2:   *Identify the sequence and interaction of processes
            within the organization.* Identify the main product
            realization processes and supporting processes
            systematically, together with the process owners
            (those responsible for the smooth operation of the
            processes). Then determine the sequence and
            interaction of these processes.

Step 3: *Describe the existing processes within the organization.* The process owners, if necessary, in coordination/ cooperation with you, should describe the processes in draft. In describing the processes you might possibly use parts of the function-based quality management system. While describing, keep in mind the scope, objectives, type and size of risks, and criteria for input and output of the processes, as well as the required resources and control. The process has to contribute to the conformity to customer and applicable regulatory requirements, the organization's own requirements, and those process owner's requirements. You could also map the process in a flowchart. Flowcharts are shorter and easier to read than written text.

Step 4: *Discuss the existing processes within the organization.* Discuss the draft process descriptions with the process owners and adapt where necessary. Then discuss the process descriptions with all employees involved as well as the owners of the preceding and following processes.

Step 5: *Determination of critical process steps.* Discuss the steps in the process that are critical, regarding the quality of the product, with the owners of the process and then with all employees concerned.

Step 6: *Controlling critical process steps.* The next step is to control the identified critical process steps. This can be done with an existing or totally new method of working.

Step 7: *Assessment against ISO 9001:2000.* Last but not least, evaluate the method of working with the requirements of ISO 9001:2000. Possible discrepancies are to be discussed with the owners of the process in question. If necessary, modify your quality management system.

Most descriptions of non-operational processes of function-based quality management systems are usable for process-based quality management systems. Possible examples are the description of the quality policy or of the execution of internal audits. These descriptions should be adjusted to the new (customer-oriented) requirements of ISO 9001:2000.

40. Which records does ISO 9001:2000 require?

You need to establish and maintain records to provide evidence of conformity to the requirements and of the effective operation of the quality management system (ANSI/ISO/ASQ Q9001-2000, para. 4.2.4). These should include:

§ in ISO 9001:2000	Record
5.6.1	Management review
6.2.2 e	Education, training, skills, and experience
7.1 d	Records to provide evidence that the realization processes and resulting product meet requirements
7.2.2	Results of the review of requirements related to the product
7.3.2	Design and development inputs
7.3.4	Results of design and development reviews and any necessary actions
7.3.5	Results of design and development verification and any necessary actions
7.3.6	Results of design and development validation and any necessary actions
7.3.7	Results of the review of design and development changes and any necessary actions
7.4.1	Results of supplier evaluations and any necessary actions arising from the review
7.5.2 d	Information on processes, necessary for validation of processes for production and service provision where the resulting output cannot be verified

continued

continued

§ in ISO 9001:2000	Record
7.5.3	Unique identification of the product where traceability is a requirement
7.5.4	Property of customer that is lost, damaged, or otherwise found to be unsuitable for use
7.6.a	Basis used for calibration or verification where no international or national measurement standards exist
7.6	Validity of previous measuring results when the equipment is found not to conform to requirements
7.6.	Results of calibration and verification
8.2.2	Results of internal audits
8.2.4	Person(s) authorizing release of product after evidence of conformity with the accepted criteria
8.3	Nature of nonconformities and any subsequent actions taken including concessions obtained
8.5.2	Results of corrective actions
8.5.3	Results of preventive actions

Examples of other records:

• Information on customers

• Information on customer satisfaction

• Logistical data

• Financial data

• Complaints

• Reports of quality costs

• Contract reviews

• Acceptable suppliers

• Information on personnel

• Performance indicators

Management Responsibility

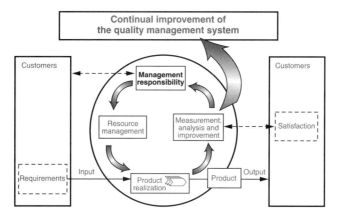

Continual improvement of the quality management system

41. Has top management's responsibility toward the customer changed?

Yes, according to ISO 9001:2000, top management is directly responsible for determining customer requirements and fulfilling them with the aim of enhancing customer satisfaction. Customer focus was also important in ISO 9001:1994, but the new standard explicitly states that top management itself is responsible for promoting customer focus at all levels of the organization.

CUSTOMER-FOCUSED ORGANIZATION

42. What is the role of top management in achieving customer focus?

With respect to customer focus, top management must:

- Communicate to the organization the importance of meeting customer (as well as statutory and regulatory) requirements (ANSI/ISO/ASQ Q9001-2000, para. 5.1)

- Ensure that customer requirements are determined and met with the aim of enhancing customer satisfaction (ANSI/ISO/ASQ Q9001-2000, para. 5.2)

Customer-focused organization is one of the eight underlying principles of quality management (see question 23).

43. How do I determine customer requirements?

You must know customer requirements well enough to be able to consistently supply products that meet them. Therefore you not only have to translate stated customer requirements into product requirements, but also nonspecified requirements that are also necessary to meet the customer satisfaction target and legal requirements (ANSI/ISO/ASQ Q9001-2000, para. 7.2). During product realization, measure and monitor whether these requirements are being met (ANSI/ISO/ASQ Q9001-2000, para. 8.2.4). This is only possible on the basis of reliable information about customer requirements. ISO 9001:2000 does not say *how* to measure customer requirements; you are free to make your own choice considering the type of organization, product, and related risks. ANSI/ISO/ASQ Q9004-2000, para. 5.2.2 can be useful.

44. Our organization rarely or never receives complaints or suggestions from our customers. Can we assume that they are satisfied?

Every organization receives feedback from customers in one way or another. Few complaints can be a good sign or mean that you have poor contact with your customers. If you never receive suggestions from customers, your contact with the customer is, most likely, not satisfactory. In that case you should try to listen more actively, to better understand their requirements. Take the initiative for this yourself. Communicate with the customer before, during, and after delivery of the product. Discuss product information, contracts, order processing (including modifications), and the customer response (including complaints). If you communicate with the customer well, you know whether or not you can assume that, in the perception of your customers, your organization has fulfilled their requirements (ANSI/ISO/ASQ Q9001-2000, para. 7.2.3. and 8.2.1).

45. If customer focus is a prime concern, then what is the position of other interested parties, such as employees? Are they not important?

Because customer focus is a prime concern in the new ISO 9001, you will, in any case, have to pay attention to the satisfaction of all your customers. In addition to customers, other interested parties are also important. ISO 9001:2000 mentions employees, suppliers, and the regulatory authorities, but does not exclude other interested parties. The main criterion of ISO 9001:2000 in deciding whether or not to consider interested parties, is your ability to meet customer and applicable regulatory requirements and to enhance customer satisfaction. So the focus is on the customer in ISO 9001:2000. ISO 9004:2000 pays attention to enhancing satisfaction of all interested parties. These include customers and end users, but also employees, shareholders, and society in terms of the community and the public affected by the organization (ANSI/ISO/ASQ Q9004-2000, para. 5.2.1).

46. What is the position of regulatory requirements in ISO 9001:2000?

ISO 9001:1994 only mentions regulatory requirements in relation to design control (ANSI/ISO/ASQ Q9001-1994, para. 4.4.4). In the new standard, addressing applicable regulatory requirements is an integral part of the quality management system (ANSI/ISO/ASQ Q9001-2000, para. 1.2). Obviously, you supply your customer with what meets the applicable regulatory requirements. For example, if you produce products for which CE marking is mandatory, you will also have to incorporate the measures necessary for this into your quality management system (see question 92).

47. What else is changing for top management?

Top management must provide evidence of its commitment to the development, implementation, and improvement of the effectiveness of the quality management system (ANSI/ISO/ASQ

Q9001-2000, para. 5.1). This can, for example, be done by creating an environment focused on realizing customer requirements (ANSI/ISO/ASQ Q9001-2000, para. 5.2).

Top management now must also ensure:

- Quality management system planning (ANSI/ISO/ASQ Q9001-2000, para. 5.4.2)

- Internal communication (ANSI/ISO/ASQ Q9001-2000, para. 5.5.3)

Top management also remains responsible for:

- Quality policy and objectives (ANSI/ISO/ASQ Q9001-2000, para. 5.3 and 5.4.1)

- Defining and communicating responsibilities, authorities and their interrelation (ANSI/ISO/ASQ Q9001-2000, para. 5.5.1)

- Review of the quality management system (ANSI/ISO/ASQ Q9001-2000, para. 5.6)

48. Are there additional requirements for quality policy?

The purpose of establishing a quality policy has remained the same in ISO 9001:2000: managers in the organization give the organization purpose and direction, and they create the environment in which employees can work together to achieve the organization's objectives. The requirements for the quality policy are formulated more specifically in ISO 9001:2000 than in ISO 9001:1994. The quality policy must be suitable for complying with customer requirements and providing evidence of management's commitment. Top management should ensure a logical relationship between policy, goals, action, and management review. Another new aspect is that the policy must include a commitment to continually improve the effectiveness of the quality management system.

According to ANSI/ISO/ASQ Q9004-2000 (para 5.3), an effectively formulated and communicated quality policy should:

- Be consistent with the vision of the organization's future

- Make quality objectives understood throughout the organization

- Demonstrate top management's commitment to quality and the provision of adequate resources for its achievement

- Promote a commitment to quality at all levels of the organization

- Address continual improvement and customer satisfaction

49. Which additional requirements apply to quality management system planning?

Additional requirements for quality management system planning are that top management:

- Shall ensure that quality objectives are established (and understood) at all relevant functions and levels within the organization (ANSI/ISO/ASQ Q9001-2000, para. 5.4.1). This is called deployment—the translation of objectives into functions and levels within the organization. This goes beyond the requirements of ISO 9001:1994, namely that the quality policy is understood, implemented, and maintained at all levels.

When establishing the quality objectives one can take into account not only the current and future requirements of the organization and the markets served, but also the results of management reviews: how good are the current processes and products, and are the customers satisfied with them?

- Shall establish measurable (new!) quality objectives: how the organization intends to implement the quality policy (ANSI/ISO/ASQ Q9001-2000, para. 5.4.1).

- Link quality planning with processes and products (ANSI/ISO/ASQ Q9001-2000, para. 4.1 and 5.4.2). This means that for each process, inputs and outputs are defined and results are measured, recorded, analyzed, and evaluated. ANSI/ISO/ASQ Q9004-2000 (para. 5.4.2) gives a list of possible inputs and outputs with regard to quality planning.

- Shall ensure that by means of quality planning, the integrity of the quality management system is maintained when the system is changed (ANSI/ISO/ASQ Q9001-2000, para. 5.4.2).

50. We have a large company with various divisions. It would be useful to appoint more than one management representative. Is this possible?

No, the management representative is one member of management. Irrespective of other responsibilities, this management team member has responsibility and authority for quality management matters (ANSI/ISO/ASQ Q9001-2000, para. 5.5.2).

51. What does the new requirement on internal communication mean?

ISO 9001:2000 includes requirements for internal communication: the organization shall ensure communication regarding the effectiveness of the quality management system (ANSI/ISO/ASQ Q9001-2000, para. 5.5.3). It is the responsibility of top management to ensure that this internal communication takes place. The management must play an active part in internal communication regarding:

- The importance of meeting customer as well as statutory and regulatory requirements (ANSI/ISO/ASQ Q9001-2000, para. 5.1)

- Quality policy (ANSI/ISO/ASQ Q9001-2000, para. 5.3)

- The responsibilities, authorities, and their interrelation (ANSI/ISO/ASQ Q9001-2000, para. 5.5.1)

The internal communication should, in any case, ensure that employees understand the quality policy and see what their role is in the processes of the quality management system. This encourages their commitment in establishing and implementing the quality objectives. For an example of internal communication, one can think of formal (existing) consultation situations where quality is a permanent or regular item on the agenda. Linked with this, it is also important to decide how to monitor any follow-up activities resulting from the consultations. In addition, things like memos, personnel newsletters, and audiovisual and electronic media can contribute to internal communication. Employees should know where to go for information on quality management in the organization.

52. Does management review change?

Yes, the requirements for the management review have become more explicit and stringent:

- For each review top management must consider whether there are reasons for changing (the method of operating) the quality management system, adapting the quality policy, and revising the objectives (ANSI/ISO/ASQ Q9001-2000, para. 5.6)

- The standard explicitly lists the minimum input for the management review: customer feedback, results of improvement actions in response to the results of previous management reviews, and consequences of the change in outside conditions, among other things (ANSI/ISO/ASQ Q9001-2000, para. 5.6.2)

- The standard explicitly lists the minimum output of the management review: improvement of the effectiveness of the quality management system itself, and product improvements related to customer requirements and resource needs (ANSI/ISO/ASQ Q9001-2000, para. 5.6.3)

6
Resource Management

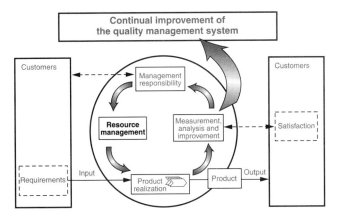

Continual improvement of the quality management system

Customers

Management responsibility

Resource management

Measurement, analysis and improvement

Customers

Satisfaction

Requirements

Input

Product realization

Product

Output

53. What does resource management mean?

Resource management means that resources which are essential to implement, maintain, and improve the effectiveness of the quality management system and to enhance customer satisfaction are identified and made available. Resource management also includes the planning of resources that will be required in the future.

Resources may include people, infrastructure, work environment, information suppliers and partners, tools, natural resources, and financial resources (ANSI/ISO/ASQ Q9004-2000, para. 6.1.1).

Resource management therefore covers tangible resources, for example work rooms, but also intangible resources such as intellectual property or experience. ISO 9001:2000 distinguishes the following types of resources:

- Human resources (ANSI/ISO/ASQ Q9001-2000, para. 6.2)

- Infrastructure (ANSI/ISO/ASQ Q9001-2000, para. 6.3)

- Work environment (ANSI/ISO/ASQ Q9001-2000, para. 6.4)

INVOLVEMENT OF PEOPLE

54. Are additional requirements for personnel included in ISO 9001:2000?

Yes, ISO 9001:2000 includes additional requirements for personnel. In the first place, personnel must be aware of the relevance and importance of quality. The same was true for the previous version of the standard, but now it is stated explicitly and focuses on promoting awareness of customer requirements (ANSI/ISO/ASQ Q9001-2000, para. 6.5.2). In addition, top management itself is responsible for this (ANSI/ISO/ASQ Q9001-2000, para. 5.1).

Subsequently, the most important requirement is that personnel must also be in a position to work with a customer focus. They must be competent and must have the necessary resources available to implement and improve processes in order to enhance customer satisfaction. Competence is the result of appropriate education, training, skills, and experience (ANSI/ISO/ASQ Q9001-2000, para. 6.2.1). The organization must determine the necessary competency level. If the personnel do not meet this level, then training must be provided or other actions must be taken. A new requirement is that the effectiveness of the offered training or other actions taken must be evaluated (ANSI/ISO/ASQ Q9001-2000, para. 6.2.2).

55. What does the new requirement about training mean?

Requirements for training were included in ANSI/ISO/ASQ Q9001-1994, para. 4.18, for personnel performing activities affecting quality. The same is true for ISO 9001:2000 (see para. 6.2.2), but added to this is the required evaluation of the effectiveness of the training provided to satisfy the competency needs. This is clarified in ANSI/ISO/ASQ Q9004-2000 (para. 6.2.2) and in ISO 10015 *Quality management—Guidelines for training*. The most important steps in providing effective training are:

Step 1: Determine for each activity the competence that is required to carry out the activity to the required quality level ("required" in terms of the current and anticipated future needs of customers and the organization, and of the legal and statutory requirements)

Step 2: Link employees to these activities, taking into account their competence

Step 3: Compare their actual competence with the required competence

Step 4: Determine (any) required supplementation of their knowledge, experience, and skills

Step 5: Determine what training is necessary to ensure this supplementation

Step 6: Provide the training

Step 7: Check whether the training was effective: does it contribute to the quality of the work?

Step 8: If necessary provide supplementary training

Step 9: Repeat this cycle again from time to time

56. Is it true that the new ISO 9000 series includes requirements for occupational health and safety?

No, not directly. The new ISO 9000 series does, however, include requirements for the work environment that may result in attention to occupational health and safety issues. The organization must ensure a work environment that is necessary to achieve conformity to product requirements (ANSI/ISO/ASQ Q9001-2000, para. 6.4). *Work environment* is defined as the set of conditions under which work is performed. These conditions include physical, social, psychological, and environmental factors (ANSI/ISO/ASQ Q9000-2000, para 3.3.4). The minimum requirements for a good work environment arise from:

• Enhancing customer satisfaction: the people must not be hindered by their work environment (ANSI/ISO/ASQ Q9001-2000, para. 6.1)

- The quality management system itself: the work environment must not hinder the employees in implementing and improving the processes of the quality management system (ANSI/ISO/ASQ Q9001-2000, para. 6.1)

- Applicable legislation (ANSI/ISO/ASQ Q9001-2000, para. 1.1)

In short, this involves the work conditions that directly affect the quality of the product. Examples of factors that may affect the work environment are: creative work methodologies to enable personnel to realize their potential, safety rules, ergonomics, temperature, noise, hygiene, and air humidity (ANSI/ISO/ASQ Q9004-2000, para. 6.4). By the way, none of this is new: ANSI/ISO/ASQ Q9001-1994, para. 4.9.b. also includes requirements for the work environment with a view to product quality.

57. Why are requirements included for the work environment? After all, ISO 9001:2000 is not about occupational health and safety management.

The focus of ISO 9001:2000 is on customer satisfaction. Their satisfaction largely depends on the supplied products. The quality of the products depends on the way in which the organization realizes these products. The work environment plays a part in this: employees must not be obstructed in their work; the work environment must invite them to provide such a performance that the customer gets what he requires, or even more than that. You have to determine, maintain, and improve these essential aspects of the work environment.

These activities form only a part of occupational health and safety management. An occupational health and safety management system focuses primarily on the employees (and on meeting the legal requirements), while a quality management system based on ISO 9001:2000 focuses on the customer. You can systematically pay attention to occupational health and safety using various national and international guidelines and specifications, such as OHSAS 18001.

58. What does ISO 9001:2000 mean by infrastructure?

Infrastructure is defined as the system of facilities, equipment and services needed for the operation of an organization (ANSI/ISO/ASQ Q9000-2000, para 3.3.3), and ISO 9001:2000 requires that the infrastructure needed to achieve conformity to the product requirements is determined and provided. ANSI/ISO/ASQ Q9001-2000, para. 6.3 mentions:

- Buildings, workspace, and associated facilities

- Process equipment (both hardware and software)

- Supporting services (such as transport or communication)

Product
Realization

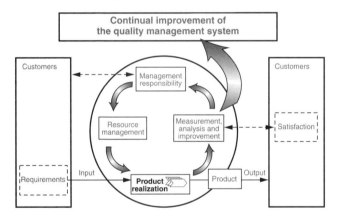

59. What does ISO 9001:2000 mean by product realization?

Product realization is the sequence of processes by which the product is realized. A process is an activity that receives inputs and converts them into outputs (ANSI/ISO/ASQ Q9001-2000, para. 0.2). The output from one process often directly forms the input for the next process. The output supplied to the customer is the product. A detailed explanation of this process approach can be found in ANSI/ISO/ASQ Q9004-2000, para. 7.1.2. In the clause on managing processes it is stated that an operating plan should be defined to manage the processes in which you can include (ANSI/ISO/ASQ Q9004-2000, para. 7.1.3.1):

- Input and output requirements for processes, such as specifications and resources needed

- Activities within the processes

- Verification and validation of processes and products

- Analysis of the process, including dependability

- Identification, assessment, and mitigation of risk

- Corrective and preventive action

- Opportunities and actions for process improvement

- Control of change

60. Does *product* also mean *service*?

Yes, in ISO 9001:2000 *product* also means *service*. A *product* is defined in ISO 9000:2000 as the result of a process, which, for example, can be a service process (see question 19).

61. What new requirements apply to product realization?

In essence, the requirements for product realization correspond with those in ISO 9001:1994, in particular with para. 4.9. The most important new requirement in clause 7 of ISO 9001:2000 relates to communication with customers about product information, enquiries, contracts and orders, and about customer feedback (including complaints) (ANSI/ISO/ASQ Q9001-2000, para. 7.2.3).

62. What does the customer communication requirement mean?

The standard focuses on meeting customer requirements and enhancing customer satisfaction (ANSI/ISO/ASQ Q9001-2000, para. 1.1). This is based on the quality management principle of customer focus, which also states that you:

- Must understand the current and future needs of your customers

- Translate these needs into requirements for the organization

- Strive even to exceed the expectations of your customers (ANSI/ISO/ASQ Q9004-2000, para. 4.3)

In view of these basic principles, it is logical that the standard requires that there must be communication with the customer. In this respect, ANSI/ISO/ASQ Q9001-2000, para. 7.2.3 clearly goes further than ANSI/ISO/ASQ Q9001-1994, para. 4.3.4. Customer communication relates to:

- Agreeing with one another about what your organization can offer to satisfy what the customer requires—you only commit yourself to supply something to the customer after you have ascertained that the customer really wants it and that your organization is able to supply it

- Product information

- Establishing a contract to supply what, when, and on what terms

- Any interim changes in contracts

- Order processing

- Communication during production and delivery

- Feedback: is the customer satisfied with what has been supplied?

- Handling any complaints (ANSI/ISO/ASQ Q9001-2000, para. 7.2.3)

63. Must the customer make all their requirements known?

For example, in the case of software products the customer often does not know how to formulate precisely what he/she needs. Good communication is certainly helpful, but often not enough. In other cases a requirement is so obvious that it will not be part of the discussion between supplier and customer. For example, anyone having a house built may assume that it will have a door. These are so-called requirements for *suitability of use*. The standard therefore indicates that you must not only take into account the stated customer requirements, but also:

- Requirements that are necessary for the specified use or intended use of the product, where known (ANSI/ISO/ASQ Q9001-2000, para. 7.2.1)

- Legal requirements (ANSI/ISO/ASQ Q9001-2000, para. 7.2.1)

It is necessary to pay attention to the broadening of the term *product* (see question 19): this not only involves customer requirements relating to the characteristics of the product to be supplied, but also those relating to availability, delivery, instructions for use, service, and guarantee provisions of the product to be supplied.

64. Are there new requirements for product design and development?

No, there are no new explicit requirements for product design and development. The same requirements more or less apply in regard to planning, inputs, outputs, review, verification, validation, and control of changes.

65. We use software to check whether the product meets the requirements. Does ISO 9001:2000 mention anything about this?

It is necessary to check the software for measuring and monitoring properties of products and the proper functioning of processes prior to use (ANSI/ISO/ASQ Q9001-2000, para. 7.6). However, this requirement is not new. ANSI/ISO/ASQ Q9001-1994, para. 4.11.1 states that software must be regularly checked to prove that it is capable of verifying the acceptability of product prior to release.

Measurement, Analysis and Improvement

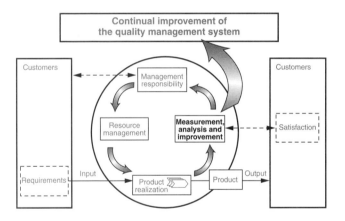

66. What does the requirement for continual improvement mean?

The requirement for continual improvement could be most clearly found in ISO 9001:1994 in the form of corrective and preventive action (ANSI/ISO/ASQ Q9001-1994, para. 4.14), and in the form of the management review (ANSI/ISO/ASQ Q9001-1994, para. 4.1.3). Although the authors of the standard had the strict intention that all measures taken together would

CONTINUAL IMPROVEMENT

lead to improvement of the quality management system and, hence, to improvement of the organization's performance, this was not stated in the standard as a requirement. This is different in ISO 9001:2000. The revised standard requires continual improvement of the effectiveness of the quality management system (ANSI/ISO/ASQ Q9001-2000, para. 8.5.1). ISO 9004:2000 provides guidance on the continual improvement of both the effectiveness and efficiency of the quality management system for those organizations that wish to go beyond the basic requirements of ISO 9001 in the pursuit of continual improvement of performance (ANSI/ISO/ASQ Q9004-2000, para. 0.3). So does ISO 9001:2000 now also require improvement of the organization's performance, or not? It is not stated as a direct requirement, however, fulfilling the requirements places you in a position to continually improve aspects of performance. When interpreting the requirement of ANSI/ISO/ASQ Q9001-2000, para. 8.5.1, we must consider the central thought behind the standard: that the organization systematically takes measures to ensure customer satisfaction by meeting customer requirements and applicable regulatory and statutory requirements (ANSI/ISO/ASQ Q9001-2000, para.1.1). The requirement that the effectiveness of the quality management system must be continually improved is linked to the enhancement of customer satisfaction (ANSI/ISO/ASQ Q9001-2000, para 1.1 b). This means that the organization will increasingly be in a better position to systematically ensure that they only enter into delivery obligations that lead to enhanced customer satisfaction. This will not automatically mean that, for example, the technical characteristics of products supplied constantly improve. The matching of product characteristics to customer wishes does, however, offer a good starting point for improving technical product characteristics or realizing other improvements, for example in the field of profitability. So we can conclude that ISO 9001:2000 does not require other improvements than that of the effectiveness of the quality management system, but by realizing this improvement, the basis for other performance improvements will be established. See also question 29.

67. Have the requirements for measurement, analysis, and improvement changed?

Measurement, analysis, and improvement in ISO 9001:1994 were aimed primarily at ensuring that agreed-upon product requirements were met. That is not different in the new standard, but now it is more focused on enhancing customer satisfaction and improving the effectiveness of the quality management system. The measurement and analysis data serve as a basis for this.

68. What are the requirements for monitoring customer satisfaction?

ISO 9001:2000 states the following about monitoring customer satisfaction:

- Monitor information related to the customer perception as to whether the organization has fulfilled customer requirements, and determine what methodologies are used to obtain and use this information (ANSI/ISO/ASQ Q9001-2000, para. 8.2.1). Depending on the type of customers, the type of product, and the related risks for the customer, you determine in what way, and with what frequency, any customer satisfaction survey can be carried out.

- Measure and monitor the processes that are necessary to meet the customer requirements by applying suitable methods. These methods shall demonstrate the ability of the processes to achieve planned results (ANSI/ISO/ASQ Q9001-2000, para. 8.2.3).

- Measure and monitor, at appropriate stages of the product realization process, the product characteristics. Verify whether these characteristics meet the customer requirements (ANSI/ISO/ASQ Q9001-2000, para. 8.2.4).

69. How can I monitor customer satisfaction?

ISO 9001:2000 does not give any instructions for measuring customer satisfaction. There is only the requirement to determine what methods are used for obtaining and using information to monitor customer satisfaction (ANSI/ISO/ASQ Q9001-2000, para. 8.2.1).

ANSI/ISO/ASQ Q9004-2000, para. 8.2.1.2 recommends measuring customer satisfaction on a continual basis. You can pay attention to the wishes, requirements, and expectations of customers with regard to, for example, quality, price, and delivery of the product.

You can also obtain information on customer satisfaction from complaints, customer panels, direct customer communication, surveys, investigations, and/or reports of consumer organizations.

70. Does the internal audit change?

A new requirement in ISO 9001:2000 is that internal audits must be conducted to determine whether the quality management system meets the requirements of ISO 9001:2000. Question 71 explains how this is determined. Internal auditors need to have good knowledge of this international standard. This was already a requirement, indirectly, in the 1994 version through the determination of the effectiveness of the quality system. Now this has been stated more directly.

In ISO 9001, ISO 9002, and ISO 9003 (1994 version), the internal audit was mainly focused on the determination of compliance with, and suitability of, the implemented quality management system. The risk in this was that non-conformance with the standard could be ignored during internal audits. Internal audits, according to ISO 9001:2000, also have the purpose of determining whether the quality management system is effectively implemented and maintained and, hence, contributes to achieving quality objectives.

Like external audits, internal audits must also be focused on the organization's processes to be sure they are in line with the process approach of the new ISO 9000 series as described in question 71.

71. Does the external audit change?

Yes, in many cases external auditing does change. ISO 9001:2000 has a different layout and a number of new requirements of which every auditor must be aware. An ISO 9001:1994 audit could be carried out by means of checklists covering the 20 subclauses in the standard and by checking to what extent the organization met these requirements. In the case of ISO 9001:2000, this approach is not so obvious. The processes now provide a basis for the auditor. For each process the auditor must check:

- How the process setup is related to the quality policy and its quality objectives

- Whether the people involved are competent and have the right resources

- Whether there is feedback of process results to the process design

- Whether the process contributes to meeting customer requirements and increasing customer satisfaction

In short, good auditors (both internal and external) will audit along the organization's processes and, in doing so, pay additional attention to completion of the PDCA cycle (Deming's Plan–Do–Check–Act cycle). This applies not only to external but also to internal audits. New points of view on audit methods and techniques are also anticipated when ISO 10011 is replaced by ISO 19011 *Guideline for auditing quality and/or environmental management systems* (publication planned for 2002). See question 72.

Certification and Transition Period

72. Will there be a new standard for auditing as well?

Yes, a new standard containing guidelines for auditing quality and/or environmental management systems is under development: ISO 19011. This standard is one of the key documents in the new ISO 9000 series and will, in accordance with the present schedule, be published in 2002. ISO 19011 will contain the following parts:

- Terms and definitions in the field of auditing

- The fundamentals of auditing

- Managing an audit program

- The process of individual audits

- Qualification for auditors

At present there are separate standards for quality and environmental management system auditing: the three parts of ISO 10011:1991 for quality management, and ISO 14010:1996, ISO 14011:1996, and ISO 14012:1996 for environmental management. These standards are very similar, which is logical because the principles, method, and objectives of auditing a quality management system and an environmental management system do not differ appreciably.

The distinction between auditing quality and environmental management systems lies, for example, in:

- The subjects the auditor looks at. Take the example of storage tanks. From the environmental point of view, the auditor will examine the technological state and related management of the storage tanks. From the quality perspective, the auditor will investigate whether or not the storage conditions affect the quality of an (intermediate) product.

- The reference framework to review the setup and proper implementation of the management system. For example ISO 14001 and environmental legislation, or ISO 9001 and customer requirements.

- The knowledge and background of the auditors, for example, an environmental technology background or experience as a product manager.

Many organizations combine quality and environmental management system audits. This saves time, and thus expense, because, for instance, organization divisions then only have to be "pestered" once by an audit team. Certification audits can also be combined on request. The most important point for concern in combined audits is the correct composition of the audit team, which should have a good mix of knowledge and experience. ISO has decided to meet this practice with the development of a new standard that is applicable to quality as well as environmental management system auditing and so can be used as a guideline for both individual and combined audits. The standard is also applicable to both internal and external audits.

ISO 19011 will replace the present ISO 10011—part 1, 2, and 3—and ISO 14010, ISO 14011, and ISO 14012.

73. My organization is currently certified on the basis of ISO 9002:1994. Now that ISO 9002 has been withdrawn, what am I supposed to do?

Organizations certified on the basis of ISO 9002:1994 either have no design and development activities or have excluded these activities from the scope of their quality management system. If design and development activities are carried out to meet your customer requirements, you must include these in your quality management system, even if that was not the case previously. If design and development activities are not present, or in other words, if your product is made on the basis of an existing design, the requirements for design and development cannot be applied and you can exclude them from the scope of your quality management system (ANSI/ISO/ASQ Q9001-2000, para. 1.2). You must then identify in the quality manual what provisions from clause 7 of ISO 9001:2000 you have excluded and why you think that is justified (ANSI/ISO/ASQ Q9001-2000, para. 4.2.2.). See also questions 4 and 5.

74. Our design and development activities are essential, but I still want to exclude these during certification on the basis of ISO 9001:2000. Is this possible?

Essential design and development activities cannot be excluded during certification on the basis of ISO 9001:2000. According to the spirit of the standard, the exclusion of design and development activities would undermine the capability of the organization to supply a product that meets customer requirements.

75. May I disregard other requirements of ISO 9001:2000 in addition to design and development activities?

For certification on the basis of ANSI/ISO/ASQ Q9001-2000, consideration for exclusion is limited to the requirements from clause 7 of the American standard, entitled *Product realization.* This means the following components:

- Planning of product realization (para. 7.1)

- Customer-related processes (para. 7.2)

- Design and development (para. 7.3)

- Purchasing (para. 7.4)

- Production and service provision (para. 7.5)

- Control of monitoring and measuring devices (para. 7.6)

If you want to exclude certain requirements for certification you must provide justification that this does not affect your ability or responsibility to provide a product that fulfills customer requirements and applicable regulatory requirements. Exclusion of requirements may arise from the nature of an organization and its product.

76. May I also add components to the quality management system that are not required in ISO 9001:2000?

You may add all the components to the quality management system that you yourself consider useful. A quality management system maintained in accordance with ISO 9001:2000 should be regarded as a minimum level of quality management. This is to be used as a basis for continual improvement. New components that you want to add may arise, for example, from preventive action, internal audits, management review, customer-satisfaction surveys, or from the conscious application of ISO 9004:2000. This guideline invites you to add components of your own choice to your quality management system, aimed at the needs and expectations of all interested parties of your organization, for example, something that is to the benefit of your own employees, the immediate environment, or the shareholders. You may also add components because a contract with a customer requires it. So, you may tailor your quality management system to your own organization taking into account specific requirements of special contracts and your own wishes. This means you direct your own path to *business excellence.*

77. I only want to become ISO 9001 certified. Do I still need to worry about ISO 9004:2000?

No, strictly speaking you don't, because ISO 9004:2000 is not intended for certification or contractual use. Whether it is sensible not to consult ISO 9004 is another matter. The heart of the review process is the idea of a *consistent pair*—ISO 9001:2000 and ISO 9004:2000.

The two standards are designed to be used in combination but you can also use them independently. The new common structure of ISO 9001:2000 and ISO 9004:2000 invites you to look beyond certification to a quality management system that really contributes to improving the performance of all the organization's activities. ISO 9004:2000 includes guidelines for general performance improvement and gives directions for a broader set of objectives for an effective and efficient quality management system (see question 13).

78. When can I have my organization certified according to the requirements of ISO 9001:2000?

Certification of quality management systems against the requirements of ISO 9001:2000 has been possible since the date the new standard was published internationally, December 15, 2000. This has been agreed upon by ISO/TC 176 (the international standards committee that is establishing the ISO 9000 standards), ISO/CASCO (the ISO committee for conformity assessment), and IAF (the International Accreditation Forum, whose members include several national accreditation councils). If your organization already has a certificate based on the 1994 version, you can have new elements of the quality management system reviewed in stages during the regular audits.

79. Can my organization still receive ISO 9001:1994 certification?

Certification of quality management systems against the requirements of ISO 9001:1994, ISO 9002:1994, or ISO 9003:1994 is still possible up to three years from the date the new standards were published, so until December 15, 2003. Certificates based on the 1994 version, however, are valid until, at the latest, three years after the publication of the ISO 9000:2000 series, so until December 15, 2003 (see question 80).

80. How long are certifications based on the ISO 9000:1994 standards valid?

Certificates normally have a validity period of a maximum of three years. For all certificates based on the 1994 version that were issued before December 15, 2000 (the publication date of the new ISO 9000 series), this maximum validity period of three years applies.

For certificates based on the 1994 version that were issued after the publication date of December 15, 2000, however, the validity period expires exactly three years after this date, on December 15, 2003. Say you receive a certificate in May 2003 based on the 1994 version, your certificate is valid until December 2003—only seven months.

It is therefore recommended that you do not wait too long to adapt your quality management system and to have this system certified on the basis of ISO 9001:2000.

81. How can one see whether an organization is certified against the requirements of the 1994 version or the 2000 version of the ISO 9000 standards?

The certificate must clearly indicate which version of the standard the certification is based on: ISO 9001:2000 or ISO 9001:1994. In addition, ISO 9002 and ISO 9003 certificates can only be based on the 1994 version, as these standards were withdrawn with the publication of the ISO 9000:2000 series.

82. What is recommended in the transition period: certification according to the requirements of the 1994 version or the 2000 version of ISO 9001?

ISO 9001:2000 sets slightly higher quality criteria than ISO 9001:1994. Your organization therefore makes a better impression with an ISO 9001:2000 certificate. In addition, ISO 9001:2000 is a better instrument for structured business management than ISO 9001:1994. Should you not yet be able to meet those requirements, then during the three year transition period you have the option of certification according to the requirements in ISO 9001:1994, ISO 9002:1994, or ISO 9003:1994.

83. If I want to quickly change over to ISO 9001:2000, how can I prepare myself?

Since December 15, 2000, the day of publication of ISO 9001:2000, it has been possible to order the standards for ISO 9000:2000, ISO 9001:2000, and ISO 9004:2000 from your national standardization body to give you guidance regarding the new requirements. In addition you can:

- Make your employees familiar with the quality management principles

- Analyze the changes in the revised standards, in particular the process model

- Determine what these changes mean for the quality management system within your organization

You can check if your national standardization body can help you here with information products. See question 87 for rapid certification based on ISO 9001:2000.

84. Do we have to adapt our quality management system to ISO 9001:2000?

As an organization you are not obliged to change your quality management system. You can, should you so desire, even go on using the old standards for many years to come, however not for certification. There are good reasons for adopting the new standards. The standards reflect new points of view on quality management systems that are shared worldwide. Your organization can benefit from these views. If you start using ISO 9001:2000, you commit yourself to continual improvement of the effectiveness of your quality management system, therefore, it is probably a good investment to bring your quality management system up to the level of the new standard. If you want to show your customers or other outside parties that you are working in accordance with ISO 9001, then it will be somewhat peculiar when customers notice you are still using the 1994 standards in a few years' time.

If you have your quality management system certified, the question is whether you will still find certification bodies willing to issue certificates based on the old (1994) standard in a few years' time (see questions 78–80).

85. How much must be changed to transition from ISO 9001:1994 to ISO 9001:2000?

In many organizations, the transition is most far-reaching in that part of the quality management system that translates the requirements of the standard into their policy interpretation by the organization (often this is called the quality manual). Procedures and work instructions must, of course, also be adapted to the new requirements of ISO 9001:2000. In many cases you do not have to change the overall structure of procedures and work instructions. If your quality management system already has a process-related setup, and if you ever started working with a quality management system because you wanted to improve the quality of your performance, then the change will probably not include very much. It is then, of course, a matter of adapting any cross-reference tables and incorporating the new requirements (mainly customer-related requirements) into the current quality management system.

The transition to the new standards is more far-reaching if you have linked your current quality management system to the structure of ISO 9001:1994 or to the structure of functions in your organization, a so-called normative or functional layout of quality management systems. In addition, if the single reason for setting up a quality management system was to obtain a certificate, you can expect a far-reaching course of change. It is recommended that you do not wait too long to introduce these changes. Question 39 explains how you can change a function-based quality management system into a process-based quality management system.

86. Will auditing be more expensive?

It is expected that the costs of audits will rise, but not spectacularly. The costs of an audit are generally controlled by guidelines from the accreditation councils that, taking into account the type of organization to be certified, associate a minimum time with each audit.

Existing accreditation guidelines for the minimum number of man-days to be spent on certification on the basis of ISO 9001:2000 remain unchanged. So for organizations that were not yet certified, the specified minimum number of audit days is the same as the number of days in the 1994 version. In an international context it has been agreed that accreditation and certification bodies may not charge additional man-days just because of the transition to ISO 9001:2000, nor may accreditation bodies charge certification bodies any additional costs because of the transition. However, since the introduction of the new standard in different organizations has different consequences for the quality management system, the repeat audit of a greatly changed quality management system cannot be carried out in the same time as that of an unchanged quality management system. In each case a review of how much additional audit time is necessary will have to be carried out. So whether the costs rise depends on the number of changes. You can minimize the chance of additional audit costs by continually improving your quality management system step by step over the three-year transition period (after the publication of ISO 9001:2000 on December 15, 2000) and by continually having this checked during regular audits. The certification body, then, does not have to charge any additional audit time for this. Apart from that, the costs of certification may differ per certification body.

87. What does the transition from ISO 9001:1994 to ISO 9001:2000 cost?

The costs of the transition from ISO 9001:1994, ISO 9002:1994, or ISO 9003:1994 to ISO 9001:2000 are difficult to express in money. They differ very much per organization. The costs can be divided into:

- Costs of deployment of own employees to adapt the quality management system

- Costs of any hiring of external consultants to adapt the system

- Costs of training or other actions taken

- Any additional audit costs (see question 86)

- Costs of buying software that, for example, monitors and analyzes customer satisfaction

If the current quality management system already has a process-based setup, and this is actively used to control and improve the processes, then not so much will have to change (except in the field of customer-related requirements) and the costs may therefore be relatively low (see question 85). The bigger your organization, the higher the costs of adapting the quality management system will be. In general, it is advised to start with far-reaching adaptations to the quality management system as soon as possible—that gives the best opportunities for normal business management to proceed unhindered.

88. Must auditors be prepared to work with ISO 9001:2000?

Yes, both external and internal auditors must be trained, not only in the new structure, content, and terminology of ISO 9000, ISO 9001, and ISO 9004, but also in the underlying quality management principles (see chapter 3). The new standards require that the auditors understand the operations and processes of organizations and that audits are conducted according to these processes (see questions 70 and 71). Additional attention is paid here in completing the PDCA cycle. Knowledge of the ISO 9000 series, the underlying process model, and the eight quality management principles is essential for both internal and external auditors. For many auditors, further training will be necessary.

89. Can I certify my organization on the basis of ISO 9004:2000, now that guidelines for self-assessment are included?

No, you cannot certify your organization on the basis of ISO 9004:2000. ISO 9004:2000 is a guideline and is not intended to be used for certification. ISO 9004:2000 gives options for improving performance. The international standardization committee for quality management (ISO/TC 176) is of the opinion that organizations themselves can best decide whether the options given for improving performance can be applied in their own organization. Only ISO 9001:2000 is intended for certification.

90. I think that our organization already meets ISO 9001:2000. I want to show this to my employees and customers with a new certification, even if my current certification has not yet expired. Do I have to have everything audited again?

With a certification based on the 2000 version you can show your customers and employees that your organization meets the requirements of ISO 9001:2000. You can contact your certification body to have your quality management system reviewed on the basis of the new standard. You can make an agreement to have this review carried out during the regular external audits. Review during the regular external audits saves you audit costs.

91. Is an ISO 9001 certification a guarantee that the organization meets the requirements of the standard?

No, that's promising too much. Certification aims to give *justified confidence* that the organization meets the requirements included in the standard. The organization already expresses that it meets these requirements and an independent third party (a certification body) has checked this, but this is no hard guarantee. Also, this is about confidence in the quality management system, not about the quality of the products supplied. It is of course true that the quality management system can only help the organization to supply products that meet customer requirements and regulatory and legal requirements.

Other Questions

92. **In the case of CE marking, European legislation refers to ISO 9001:1994, ISO 9002:1994, and ISO 9003:1994. What happens to this now that only ISO 9001:2000 remains?**

This is an important problem for organizations that make products for which CE marking is mandatory. The European standards institute (CEN) has planned to solve this. ISO 9001:2000 has been taken over and reissued as EN-ISO 9001:2000, after approval by the CEN members (the national standards institutions in the countries of the European Union, Iceland, Norway, Switzerland, and the Czech Republic). The foreword to this European standard summarizes which modules of CE marking refer to ISO 9000:1994 standards. Module E refers to ISO 9003:1994, module D refers to ISO 9002:1994, and module H refers to ISO 9001:1994. Organizations involved with ISO 9002:1994 and ISO 9003:1994, and that will work with ISO 9001:2000, may exclude specific requirements from ISO 9001:2000 as far as conformity with these modules is concerned. For module H, all the requirements from ISO 9001:2000 apply. Only the requirements from clause 7 of ISO 9001:2000 can be considered for such exclusion.

In short, it looks as though the modules in the guidelines for CE marking will provisionally be maintained and that, via the foreword to the standard, simple instructions will be given for organizations involved with the modules of CE marking as to how they must use the new ISO 9001:2000. See also questions 73 and 74.

93. Our organization has just started reorganizing. Should we wait to modify our quality management system?

No unequivocal answer can be given to this question. The choice of whether or not to adapt immediately will differ per organization and stage of reorganization. In the answer below, arguments both for and against are explained. In principle, it is recommended that you immediately carry out the adaptation of the quality management system during the reorganization. In particular the discussions about the new tasks, responsibilities, and authorities can contribute to a better point of view of the functioning of an organization and the quality management system. Another important reason not to wait to adapt is that, after reorganization projects, the willingness of employees to change has often decreased. Employees can get tired of change and this can hinder the adaptation of the quality management system. Some understanding of the uncertain situation in which many employees find themselves during reorganization is desirable. The implementation of changes can also take longer due to the reorganization. The quality management principles (see chapter 3) may give guidance for reorganization and help to anchor the measures in the organization.

Reasons can also be mentioned for waiting to adapt the quality management system during reorganization. Reorganization requires a lot of time and attention. As the adaptation of the quality management system also takes a lot of time and attention, it is sometimes difficult to combine the two. Also, usually not everyone is pleased about reorganization and that can be a bad starting point for adapting the quality management system.

94. We are a small consultancy bureau in construction services. Can the new ISO 9001 also be beneficial to us?

The ISO 9000 series, and hence the new ISO 9001, can be used for organizations of any size. Whether your organization is big or small, ISO 9001:2000 can be applied. ISO 9001:2000 can also be used for separate divisions of an organization. Also, the new ISO 9001 can be applied for all sectors and product categories. The distinction that was made in the 1994 version of the ISO 9000 series, for example ISO 9004-2 *Quality management and quality system elements. Part 2: Guidelines for services* has disappeared (see question 1).

In short, whether your organization is active in construction services, consultancy, healthcare, or any other field, ISO 9001:2000 can be applied.

95. What does ISO mean?

ISO is the International Organization for Standardization. "ISO" is not an acronym but a name derived from the Greek word *isos,* meaning equal. This Greek word is the basis of the prefix "iso-" that is found in many scientific terms, for example isobar, a line on a map that links points with the same air pressure. ISO is also the prefix of the international standards that are published by ISO, for example ISO 9001 and ISO 14001.

ISO is the official international standards organization, in addition to the International Electrotechnical Commission (IEC, for standardization in the electrotechnical field) and the International Telecommunication Union (ITU, for standardization in the field of telecommunications).

ISO is a private organization. The members of ISO are national standardization bodies, such as NEN for the Netherlands, SA for Australia, ANSI for the USA, BSI for the United Kingdom, and DIN for Germany. At present, ISO has some 130 members from the same number of countries (for every country can only have one member of ISO, that member being the most representative standardization body in that country). ISO develops international standards. This work is carried out in so-called technical committees (TCs) whose secretariats are headed by members of the ISO. For example ISO/TC 176 *Quality management and quality assurance* is responsible for the ISO 9000 family for quality management, and the secretariat of this is in the hands of the Canadian Standards Association (CSA). The ISO itself has a relatively small coordinating secretariat in Geneva.

The ISO standards are created with the contribution of all the members of ISO. Delegated national experts in working groups draw up drafts for standards which then, via various voting and comment rounds among the ISO members, lead to final international standards or other ISO publications, such as technical reports (TR's) or technical specifications (TS's). In ISO/TC 176 about 350 experts from 60 different countries work on the standards for quality management systems.

96. Are only ISO 9001 certificates that bear the logo of a national accreditation council accepted?

A certificate that shows the logo of a national accreditation council is a so-called accredited certificate. Certification bodies that have been accredited may in fact only issue accredited certificates. Accredited certification bodies may put the logo of the accreditation council on the certificate to be issued. Accreditation councils monitor the quality of the certification and the competence of certification auditors. This happens on the basis of regular accreditation audits. This, in fact, requires achieving an internationally agreed-upon level of quality management (based on ISO standards). Finally, there may be certification bodies that carry out certification to ISO 9001 without being recognized themselves by the national accreditation body. The question lies in what value these certificates have.

97. What is accreditation?

Accreditation is the means that an authoritative body (such as the ANSI–RAB National Accreditation Program) uses to give formal recognition that an organization (such as a certification/registration body) is competent to carry out specific tasks. Accreditation, which is strictly voluntary, provides assurance to a registrar's customers that the registrar continues to operate according to internationally accepted criteria.

In the ISO 9000 field, accreditation relates to the work of RAB in providing oversight of the activities of quality management system registrars. Accreditation bodies approve registrars as competent to carry out ISO 9000 registration of quality management systems in specified business sectors.

Most national accreditation bodies are associated in an international forum of accreditation bodies, the IAF. The members of the IAF assess one another by means of peer reviews based on the requirements of ISO/IEC Guide 61:1996. Herewith, the credibility, reliability, and mutual equivalence of all certification bodies is guaranteed through approval by the accreditation body of the respective country.

98. I want to make my certification public. Can I use the ISO logo for this, or must I do something else?

Obtaining an ISO 9000 certificate is a milestone. You naturally want to make this result known to your customers and other relations. You can agree with the certification body that grants you the ISO 9001 certificate to use *their* logo, *not* the ISO logo, on your advertising statements, for example on letterheads, in brochures, in advertisements, or on company cars. This way you can show that your organization owns a certificate on the basis of ISO 9001 and by whom you were certified.

In practice it is found that many organizations make errors in promoting the certificate. A few examples:

- Wrong: "This manual was approved by certification body X"

  Right: "The quality management system was approved by certification body X"

- Wrong: "ISO-certified"—ISO, the International Organization for Standardization, after all does not issue certificates; the core activity of the ISO is the development of standards (see question 95)

  Right: "ISO 9001-certified" or "certified on the basis of ISO 9001" or "certified according to the requirements of ISO 9001:2000"

- Wrong: marking on a product "ISO 9001-certified"—this incorrectly suggests that the product is certified, while the certificate relates to the quality management system

- Wrong: use of the ISO logo

  Right: you can use the logo of your certification body, if the certification body agrees

99. Can our organization be certified by the national standardization body?

In many countries, organizations cannot be certified by the national standardization body. These standardization bodies are not certification bodies, but bodies just for issuing standards. Many other standardization bodies, however, have a certification department, such as BSI in the United Kingdom. Some standardization bodies also perform accreditation activities, for example the Russian Federation. ISO 9000 certificates are issued by certification bodies that are accredited (recognized) in the United States by the Registrar Accreditation Board (RAB). See questions 96 and 97.

100. What is the relationship between the national standardization body and ISO?

The national standardization body is generally a member of ISO. As a member of ISO, national standardization bodies can participate in all the international standardization activities that are important for the member country. This certainly applies for standardization in the field of quality management. Through the national standardization body, interested parties can exert influence on the development of standards from the ISO 9000 family. This can be accomplished by participating in the national standardization committee on quality management that establishes the national (for example, American) points of view regarding developments in standards and draft standards from the ISO 9000 family. This national standardization committee also decides on the national delegation to international ISO meetings. Parties can also choose to have a more direct influence on the content of the standards by participating directly in international working groups. The national standards committee nominates experts for international working groups. The national standardization body appoints the actual participants from the list of nominees.

We hope that this 100 questions book meets your expectations and that you are satisfied. We have added this extra question because we always endeavor to exceed our customers' expectations.

101. Is ISO 9001:2000 better-aligned with ISO 14001?

ISO 9001:2000 is better-aligned than ISO 9001:1994 with ISO 14001, the international standard with requirements for environmental management systems. This applies both to the requirements for the different system elements and to the structure of both standards. ISO 9001:2000 is now more clearly aimed at continual improvement of the quality management system with the focus of being better able to improve customer satisfaction. This is entirely comparable with the requirement in ISO 14001 to continually improve the environmental management system with a view to providing environmental performance that is socially desirable. Also, the structure of the standards now shows more relationship: the most important requirements in both ISO 9001:2000 and ISO 14001 are structured as a control and improvement cycle, while in the 1994 version of ISO 9001 such a structure is missing. The main difference in content is, of course, that ISO 14001 focuses on the environmental aspects of business management that lead to good environmental performance, while ISO 9001:2000 focuses on the control and improvement of activities that are critical for the realization of products that meet customer requirements, leading to the satisfaction of the customer. The way in which this is structured in the organization, however, shows a lot of similarity. It is expected that the integration of quality and environmental management systems will become easier thanks to the new standards. Organizations that already combine ISO 9001:1994 and ISO 14001 will not have too much difficulty in moving over from ISO 9001:1994 to ISO 9001:2000. The connection between ISO 9001:2000 and ISO 14001 is, after all, certainly not yet complete.

Appendix 1

Abbreviations Used

ANSI   American National Standards Institute

ASQ   American Society for Quality

BS   British Standard

BSI   British Standards Institution

CASCO   Conformity Assessment Committee of the ISO

CD   Committee Draft

CEN   Comité Européen de Normalisation

CSA   Canadian Standards Association

DIN   Deutsches Institut für Normung
(German Standards Institute)

EN   European Standard

EN-ISO   European adopted ISO standard

IAF   International Accreditation Forum

IEC   International Electrotechnical Commission

IS   International Standard

ISO	International Organization for Standardization
ITU	International Telecommunication Union
NEN	Nederlandse norm (Dutch Standard)/Dutch Standardization Institute
OHSAS	Occupational Health and Safety Assessment Series
PDCA	Plan–Do–Check–Act (Deming cycle)
RAB	Registrar Accreditation Board
SA	Social Accountability
SC	Subcommittee
TC	Technical Committee
TR	Technical Report
TS	Technical Specification
WG	Working Group

Appendix 2

List of Standards in the ISO 9000 Family

THE ISO 9000 SERIES
(THE CORE OF THE ISO 9000 FAMILY)

ANSI/ISO/ASQ Q9000-2000 *Quality management systems—Fundamentals and vocabulary*

ANSI/ISO/ASQ Q9001-2000 *Quality management systems—Requirements*

ANSI/ISO/ASQ Q9004-2000 *Quality management systems—Guidelines for performance improvements*

BSR/ISO/ASQ QE19011 DIS *Guidelines for quality and/or environmental management system auditing.*[1]

OTHER PUBLICATIONS IN THE
ISO 9000 FAMILY

ANSI/ISO/ASQC A8402-1994 *Standards for quality management and quality assurance—Vocabulary*

ANSI/ISO/ASQC Q9000-1-1994 *Guidelines for selection and use*

---

[1]This standard will, upon publication, replace ISO 10011 part 1, 2, and 3.

ANSI/ISO/ASQ Q9000-2-1997 *Generic guidelines for the application of ISO 9001, ISO 9002 and ISO 9003*

ANSI/ISO/ASQ Q9000-3-1997 *Guidelines for the application of ISO 9001:1994 to the development, supply, installation and maintenance of software*

ISO 9000-4:1993 *Guide to dependability programme management*

ANSI/ISO/ASQC Q9002-1994 *Model for quality assurance in production, installation and servicing*

ANSI/ISO/ASQC Q9003-1994 *Model for quality assurance in final inspection and test*

ANSI/ISO/ASQC Q9004-1-1994 *Quality management and quality system elements—Guidelines*

ANSI/ISO/ASQC Q9004-2-1991 *Guidelines for services*

ANSI/ISO/ASQC Q9004-3-1994 *Guidelines for processed materials*

ANSI/ISO/ASQC Q9004-4-1994 *Guidelines for quality improvement*

ISO 10005:1996 *Quality management—Guidelines for quality plans*

ANSI/ISO/ASQ Q10006-1997 *Quality management— Guidelines for quality in project management*

ANSI/ISO/ASQC Q10007-1995 *Quality management— Guidelines for configuration management*

ANSI/ISO/ASQC Q10011-1-1994 *Guidelines for auditing quality systems—Part 1: Auditing*

ANSI/ISO/ASQC Q10011-2-1994 *Guidelines for auditing quality systems—Part 2: Qualification criteria for quality systems auditors*

ANSI/ISO/ASQC Q10011-3-1994 *Guidelines for auditing quality systems—Part 3: Management of audit programmes*

ISO 10012-1:1992 *Quality assurance requirements for measuring equipment—Part 1: Meteorological confirmation system for measuring equipment*

ISO 10012-2:1997 *Quality assurance requirements for measuring equipment—Part 2: Control of measurement processes*

ISO/DIS 10012:2001 *Measurement control systems* (revision of ISO 10012-1:1992 and ISO 10012-2:1997)

ISO/TR 10013:2001 *Guidelines for developing quality management system documentation*

ISO/TR 10014:1998 *Guidelines for managing the economics of quality*

ANSI/ISO/ASQ Q10015-2001 *Quality management— Guidelines for training*

ISO/TR 10017:1999 *Guide to the application of Statistical Techniques for ISO 9001:1994*

Appendix 3

Correspondence between ISO 9001:2000 and ISO 14001:1996

ISO 9001:2000			ISO 14001:1996
Introduction			**Introduction**
General	0.1		
Process approach	0.2		
Relationship with ISO 9004	0.3		
Compatibility with other management systems	0.4		
Scope	1	1	**Scope**
General	1.1		
Application	1.2		
Normative reference	2	2	**Normative references**
Terms and definitions	3	3	**Definitions**
Quality management system	4	4	**Environmental management system requirements**
General requirements	4.1	4.1	General requirements
Documentation requirements	4.2		
General	4.2.1	4.4.4	Environmental management system documentation
Quality manual	4.2.2	4.4.4	Environmental management system documentation
Control of documents	4.2.3	4.4.5	Document control
Control of records	4.2.4	4.5.3	Records

continued

ISO 9001:2000			ISO 14001:1996	
Management responsibility	**5**	4.4.1	Structure and responsibility	
Management commitment	5.1	4.2	Environmental policy	
		4.4.1	Structure and responsibility	
Customer focus	5.2	4.3.1	Environmental aspects	
		4.3.2	Legal and other requirements	
Quality policy	5.3	4.2	Environmental policy	
Planning	5.4	4.3	Planning	
Quality objectives	5.4.1	4.3.3	Objectives and targets	
Quality management system planning	5.4.2	4.3.4	Environmental management programme(s)	
Responsibility, authority and communication	5.5	4.1	General requirements	
Responsibility and authority Management representative	5.5.1 5.5.2	4.4.1	Structure and responsibility	
Internal communication	5.5.3	4.4.3	Communication	
Management review General Review input Review output	5.6 5.6.1 5.6.2 5.6.3	4.6	Management review	
Resource management Provision of resources Human resources General	**6** 6.1 6.2 6.2.1	4.4.1	Structure and responsibility	
Competence, awareness and training	6.2.2	4.4.2	Training, awareness and competence	
Infrastructure Work environment	6.3 6.4	4.4.1	Structure and responsibility	
Product realization	**7**	**4.4** 4.4.6	**Implementation and operation** Operational control	
Planning of realization processes Customer-related processes	7.1 7.2	4.4.6	Operational control	
Determination of requirements related to the product	7.2.1	4.3.1 4.3.2 4.4.6	Environmental aspects Legal and other requirements Operational control	

continued

ISO 9001:2000		ISO 14001:1996	
Review of requirements related to the product	7.2.2	4.4.6	Operational control
		4.3.1	Environmental aspects
Customer communication	7.2.3	4.4.3	Communications
Design and development	7.3		
Design and development planning	7.3.1	4.4.6	Operational control
Design and development inputs	7.3.2		
Design and development outputs	7.3.3		
Design and development review	7.3.4		
Design and development verification	7.3.5		
Design and development validation	7.3.6		
Control of design and development changes	7.3.7		
Purchasing	7.4	4.4.6	Operational control
Purchasing process	7.4.1		
Purchasing information	7.4.2		
Verification of purchased product	7.4.3		
Production and service provision	7.5	4.4.6	Operational control
Control of production and service provision	7.5.1		
Validation of processes for production and service provision	7.5.2		
Identification and traceability	7.5.3		
Customer property	7.5.4		
Preservation of product	7.5.5		
Control of monitoring and measuring devices	7.6	4.5.1	Monitoring and measurement
Measurement, analysis and improvement	**8**	4.5	Checking and corrective action
General	8.1	4.5.1	Monitoring and measurement
Monitoring and measurement	8.2		
Customer satisfaction	8.2.1		
Internal audit	8.2.2	4.5.4	Environmental management system audit

continued

continued

ISO 9001:2000			ISO 14001:1996
Monitoring and measurement of processes	8.2.3	4.5.1	Monitoring and measurement
Monitoring and measurement of product	8.2.4		
Control of nonconforming product	8.3	4.5.2	Nonconformance and corrective and preventive action
		4.4.7	Emergency preparedness and response
Analysis of data	8.4	4.5.1	Monitoring and measurement
Improvement	8.5	4.2	Environmental policy
Continual improvement	8.5.1	4.3.4	Environmental management programme(s)
Corrective action	8.5.2	4.5.2	Nonconformance and corrective and preventive action
Preventive action	8.5.3		

Source: ANSI/ISO/ASQ Q9001-2000 Table A.1

Appendix 4

Correspondence between ISO 14001:1996 and ISO 9001:2000

ISO 14001:1996		ISO 9001:2000	
Introduction	–	**0** 0.1 0.2 0.3 0.4	**Introduction** General Process approach Relationship with ISO 9004 Compatibility with other management systems
Scope	1	**1** 1.1 1.2	**Scope** General Application
Normative references	2	**2**	**Normative reference**
Definitions	3	**3**	**Terms and definitions**
Environmental management system requirements	4	**4**	**Quality management system**
General requirements	4.1	4.1 5.5 5.5.1	General requirements Responsibility, authority and communication Responsibility and authority
Environmental policy	4.2	5.1 5.3 8.5	Management commitment Quality policy Improvement

continued

ISO 14001:1996			ISO 9001:2000
Planning	4.3	5.4	Planning
Environmental aspects	4.3.1	5.2	Customer focus
		7.2.1	Determination of requirements related to the product
		7.2.2	Review of requirements related to the product
Legal and other requirements	4.3.2	5.2	Customer focus
		7.2.1	Determination of requirements related to the product
Objectives and targets	4.3.3	5.4.1	Quality objectives
Environmental manage-ment programme(s)	4.3.4	5.4.2	Quality management system planning
		8.5.1	Continual improvement
Implementation and operation	4.4	**7**	**Product realization**
		7.1	Planning of product realization
Structure and responsibility	4.4.1	**5**	**Management responsibility**
		5.1	Management commitment
		5.5.1	Responsibility and authority
		5.5.2	Management representative
		6	**Resource management**
		6.1	Provisions of resources
		6.2	Human resources
		6.2.1	General
		6.3	Infrastructure
		6.4	Work environment
Training, awareness and competence	4.4.2	6.2.2	Competence, awareness and training
Communication	4.4.3	5.5.3	Internal communication
		7.2.3	Customer communication
Environmental management system documentation	4.4.4	4.2	Documentation requirements
		4.2.1	General
		4.2.2	Quality manual
Document control	4.4.5	4.2.3	Control of documents

continued

ISO 14001:1996		ISO 9001:2000	
Operational control	4.4.6	**7**	**Product realization**
		7.1	Planning of product realization
		7.2	Customer-related processes
		7.2.1	Determination of requirements related to the product
		7.2.2	Review of requirements related to the product
		7.3	Design and development
		7.3.1	Design and development planning
		7.3.2	Design and development inputs
		7.3.3	Design and development outputs
		7.3.4	Design and development review
		7.3.5	Design and development verification
		7.3.6	Design and development validation
		7.3.7	Control of design and development changes
		7.4	Purchasing
		7.4.1	Purchasing process
		7.4.2	Purchasing information
		7.4.3	Verification of purchased products
		7.5	Production and service provisions
		7.5.1	Control of production and service provision
		7.5.3	Identification and traceability
		7.5.4	Customer property
		7.5.5	Preservation of product
		7.5.2	Validation of processes for production and service provision
Emergency preparedness and response	4.4.7	8.3	Control of nonconforming product
Checking and corrective action	4.5	**8**	**Measurement, analysis and improvement**

continued

continued

ISO 14001:1996			ISO 9001:2000
Monitoring and measurement	4.5.1	7.6	Control of monitoring and measuring devices
		8.1	General
		8.2	Monitoring and measurement
		8.2.1	Customer satisfaction
		8.2.3	Monitoring and measurement of processes
		8.2.4	Monitoring and measurement of product
		8.4	Analysis of data
Nonconformance and corrective and preventive action	4.5.2	8.3	Control of nonconforming product
		8.5.2	Corrective action
		8.5.3	Preventive action
Records	4.5.3	4.2.4	Control of records
Environmental management system audit	4.5.4	8.2.2	Internal audit
Management review	4.6	5.6	Management review
		5.6.1	General
		5.6.2	Review input
		5.6.3	Review output

Source: ANSI/ISO/ASQ Q9001-2000 Table A.2

Appendix 5

Correspondence between ISO 9001:1994 and ISO 9001:2000

ISO 9001:1994	ISO 9001:2000
1 Scope	1
2 Normative reference	2
3 Definitions	3
4 Quality system requirements (title only)	
4.1 Management responsibility (title only) 4.1.1 Quality policy 4.1.2 Organization (title only) 4.1.2.1 Responsibility and authority 4.1.2.2 Resources 4.1.2.3 Management representative 4.1.3 Management review	 5.1 + 5.3 + 5.4.1 5.5.1 6.1 + 6.2.1 5.5.2 5.6.1 + 8.5.1
4.2 Quality system (title only) 4.2.1 General 4.2.2 Quality system procedures 4.2.3 Quality planning	 4.1 + 4.2.2 4.2.1 5.4.2 + 7.1
4.3 Contract review (title only) 4.3.1 General 4.3.2 Review 4.3.3 Amendment to a contract 4.3.4 Records	 5.2 + 7.2.1 + 7.2.2 + 7.2.3 7.2.2 7.2.2

continued

ISO 9001:1994	ISO 9001:2000
4.4 Design control (title only)	
4.4.1 General	
4.4.2 Design and development planning	7.3.1
4.4.3 Organizational and technical interfaces	7.3.1
4.4.4 Design input	7.2.1 + 7.3.2
4.4.5 Design output	7.3.3
4.4.6 Design review	7.3.4
4.4.7 Design verification	7.3.5
4.4.8 Design validation	7.3.6
4.4.9 Design changes	7.3.7
4.5 Document and data control (title only)	
4.5.1 General	4.2.3
4.5.2 Document and data approval and issue	4.2.3
4.5.3 Document and data changes	4.2.3
4.6 Purchasing (title only)	
4.6.1 General	
4.6.2 Evaluation of subcontractors	7.4.1
4.6.3 Purchasing data	7.4.2
4.6.4 Verification of purchased product	7.4.3
4.7 Control of customer-supplied product	7.5.4
4.8 Product identification and traceability	7.5.3
4.9 Process control	6.3 + 6.4 + 7.5.1 + 7.5.2
4.10 Inspection and testing (title only)	
4.10.1 General	7.1 + 8.1
4.10.2 Receiving inspection and testing	7.4.3 + 8.2.4
4.10.3 In-process inspection and testing	8.2.4
4.10.4 Final inspection and testing	8.2.4
4.10.5 Inspection and test records	7.5.3 + 8.2.4
4.11 Control of inspection, measuring and test equipment (title only)	
4.11.1 General	7.6
4.11.2 Control procedure	7.6
4.12 Inspection and test status	7.5.3
4.13 Control of nonconforming product (title only)	
4.13.1 General	8.3
4.13.2 Review and disposition of nonconforming product	8.3

continued

continued

ISO 9001:1994	ISO 9001:2000
4.14 Corrective and preventive action (title only) 4.14.1 General 4.14.2 Corrective action 4.14.3 Preventive action	 8.5.2 + 8.5.3 8.5.2 8.5.3
4.15 Handling, storage, packaging, preservation and delivery (title only) 4.15.1 General 4.15.2 Handling 4.15.3 Storage 4.15.4 Packaging 4.15.5 Preservation 4.15.6 Delivery	 7.5.5 7.5.5 7.5.5 7.5.5 7.5.5 7.5.1
4.16 Control of quality records	4.2.4
4.17 Internal quality audits	8.2.2 + 8.2.3
4.18 Training	6.2.2
4.19 Servicing	7.5.1
4.20 Statistical techniques (title only) 4.20.1 Identification of need 4.20.2 Procedures	 8.1 + 8.2.3 + 8.2.4 + 8.4 8.1 + 8.2.3 + 8.2.4 + 8.4

Source: ANSI/ISO/ASQ Q9001-2000 Table B.1

Appendix 6

Correspondence between ISO 9001:2000 and ISO 9001:1994

ISO 9001:2000	ISO 9001:1994
1 Scope 1.1 General 1.2 Application	1
2 Normative references	2
3 Terms and definitions	3
4 Quality management system (title only)	
4.1 General requirements	4.2.1
4.2 Documentation requirements (title only) 4.2.1 General 4.2.2 Quality manual 4.2.3 Control of documents 4.2.4 Control of records	 4.2.2 4.2.1 4.5.1 + 4.5.2 + 4.5.3 4.16
5 Management responsibility (title only)	
5.1 Management commitment	4.1.1
5.2 Customer focus	4.3.2
5.3 Quality policy	4.1.1

continued

ISO 9001:2000	ISO 9001:1994
5.4 Planning (title only) 5.4.1 Quality objectives 5.4.2 Quality management system planning	4.1.1 + 4.2.1 4.2.3
5.5 Responsibility, authority and communication (title only) 5.5.1 Responsibility and authority 5.5.2 Management representative 5.5.3 Internal communication	 4.1.2.1 4.1.2.3
5.6 Management review (title only) 5.6.1 General 5.6.2 Review input 5.6.3 Review output	 4.1.3
6 Resource management (title only)	
6.1 Provision of resources	4.1.2.2
6.2 Human resources (title only) 6.2.1 General 6.2.2 Competence, awareness and training	 4.1.2.2 4.18
6.3 Infrastructure	4.9
6.4 Work environment	4.9
7 Product realization (title only)	
7.1 Planning of product realization	4.2.3 + 4.10.1

7.2 Customer-related processes (title only)
7.2.1 Determination of requirements
  related to the product
7.2.2 Review of requirements related
  to the product
7.2.3 Customer communication
	
	4.3.2 + 4.4.4
	
	4.3.2 + 4.3.3 + 4.3.4
	
	4.3.2

7.3 Design and development (title only) 7.3.1 Design and development planning 7.3.2 Design and development inputs 7.3.3 Design and development outputs 7.3.4 Design and development review 7.3.5 Design and development verification 7.3.6 Design and development validation 7.3.7 Control of design and development changes	 4.4.2 + 4.4.3 4.4.4 4.4.5 4.4.6 4.4.7 4.4.8 4.4.9
7.4 Purchasing (title only) 7.4.1 Purchasing process 7.4.2 Purchasing information 7.4.3 Verification of purchased product	 4.6.2 4.6.3 4.6.4 + 4.10.2

continued

continued

ISO 9001:2000	ISO 9001:1994
7.5 Production and service provision (title only)	
7.5.1 Control of production and service provision	4.9 + 4.15.6 + 4.19
7.5.2 Validation of processes for production and service provision	4.9
7.5.3 Identification and traceability	4.8 + 4.10.5 + 4.12
7.5.4 Customer property	4.7
7.5.5 Preservation of product	4.15.2 + 4.15.3 + 4.15.4 + 4.15.5
7.6 Control of monitoring and measuring devices	4.11.1 + 4.11.2
8 Measurement, analysis and improvement (title only)	
8.1 General	4.10.1 + 4.20.1 + 4.20.2
8.2 Monitoring and measurement (title only)	
8.2.1 Customer satisfaction	
8.2.2 Internal audit	4.17
8.2.3 Monitoring and measurement of processes	4.17 + 4.20.1 + 4.20.2
8.2.4 Monitoring and measurement of product	4.10.2 + 4.10.3 + 4.10.4 + 4.10.5 + 4.20.1 + 4.20.2
8.3 Control of nonconforming product	4.13.1 + 4.13.2
8.4 Analysis of data	4.20.1 + 4.20.2
8.5 Improvement (title only)	
8.5.1 Continual improvement	4.1.3
8.5.2 Corrective action	4.14.1 + 4.14.2
8.5.3 Preventive action	4.14.1 + 4.14.3

Source: ANSI/ISO/ASQ Q9001-2000 Table B.2

Authors

Louise Bergenhenegouwen is a standardization consultant for quality and environmental management systems for NEN Consulting Services Management Systems at the Netherlands Standardization Institute. She was closely involved in the development of the new ISO 9000:2000 series and coordinates all the operations within the ISO 9000 campaign. Ms. Bergenhenegouwen can regularly be found as a speaker at symposia, congresses, and courses on developments within the ISO 9000 series. Until July 1999 she was employed as quality manager and management systems consultant at a consultancy office.

Annemarie de Jong is a standardization consultant with the Netherlands Standardization Institute. She coordinates the Dutch standardization operations in the field of quality management for NEN Consulting Services Management Systems. Ms. de Jong is secretary of the Dutch Quality Management Standardization Committee and of the ISO subcommittee supporting technologies in the field of quality management (ISO/TC 176/SC 3). She also coordinates the involvement of the quality platform of the Netherlands Standardization Institute in these operations.

Henk J. de Vries is associate professor of standardization at the Erasmus University, Faculteit Bedrijfskunde Rotterdam School of Management. He is also senior standardization consultant with the Netherlands Standardization Institute. Mr. de Vries has wide experience with standardization and management systems as a consultant, researcher, teacher, and author of various books and other publications. He recently received his PhD after publishing his thesis, "Standardization—A Business Approach to the Role of National Standardization Organizations."

Index